The Gift of Love

Freely Given, Freely Receive

Enoch Adejare Adeboye

Largo, MD, USA

Copyright © 2014 Enoch Adejare Adeboye

All rights reserved under the international copyright law. No part of this book may be reproduced or transmitted in any form or by any means, electronic or mechanical, including photocopying, recording, or by any information storage and retrieval system, without the express, written permission of the author or the publisher. The exception is reviewers, who may quote brief passages in a review.

Christian Living Books, Inc.
P. O. Box 7584
Largo, MD 20792
christianlivingbooks.com
We bring your dreams to fruition.

ISBN 9780971176034

Unless otherwise marked, all Scripture quotations are taken from the Holy Bible, New International Version ®. NIV®. Copyright © 1973, 1978, 1984 by International Bible Society. Used by permission of Zondervan. All rights reserved.

Scripture quotations marked NKJV are taken from the New King James Version®. Copyright © 1982 by Thomas Nelson, Inc. Used by permission. All rights reserved.

Contents

Introduction 1
Chapter 1 – Love Gives 5
Chapter 2 – Love Gives Life 13
Chapter 3 – Love Bestows Blessings 23
Chapter 4 – Love Fuels Friendship 29
Chapter 5 – Love Lends Heritage 35
Chapter 6 – Love Fosters Freedom 43
Chapter 7 – Love Bequeths Benefits 49
Chapter 8 – Love Gives Generously 59
Chapter 9 – Love Gives Victory 67
Chapter 10 – Love Gives Purposefully 71
Chapter 11 – Love Gives Absolutely 77
Chapter 12 – Love Makes a Way 91
Chapter 13 – The Greatest Joy 95
Chapter 14 – Accept the Love of God 99
About the Author 111

Introduction

Jesus Christ is a Gift with many parts. It's like getting a Christmas basket, filled with many presents. There are so many things loaded in this single gift God gave us. To illustrate this point, we can look at the life of the leper in Matthew's Gospel:

> *When he came down from the mountainside, large crowds followed him. A man with leprosy came and knelt before him and said, "Lord, if you are willing, you can make me clean. Jesus reached out his hand and touched the man. 'I am willing," he said. "Be clean!" Immediately he was cured of his leprosy. (Matthew 8:1-3)*

Here we find someone who received Jesus Christ and through Him, was blessed with several gifts. Leprosy was not only deadly, but it was also contagious. This leper was a "carrier of death". The day the leper crossed paths with Jesus Christ, he caught up with the "Carrier of Life" and there was a divine exchange. The "Life" in Jesus Christ swallowed up "death" in the man and he became a carrier of the testimony of life.

Another way to look at this is to consider that the life of this leper was at a dead end. He could not trade, marry, work or live among people. When a man, whose life hits a dead end, comes across Jesus Christ, he will discover that in the same Jesus, he finds the Way.

> *Jesus answered, 'I am the way and the truth and the life. No one comes to the Father except through me.*
> *(John 14:6)*

If your life is at a dead end and you receive Jesus as your Lord and Savior, suddenly, ways and means become available to you because He is the Way.

JOY UNSPEAKABLE

The leper was a very lonely man. When a lonely man comes in contact with Jesus Christ, He finds a Friend. Hebrews 13:5 tells us that He will never leave us or forsake us. This leper must have been a sorrowful man. If such a man comes across Jesus Christ, he meets with the joy generator. Consider the words of Jesus:

> *I have told you this so that my joy may be in you and that your joy may be complete. (John 15:11)*

When you give your life to Jesus Christ, you will begin to know the meaning of joy. If you are born-again and you do not have joy bubbling in your life, something must be wrong with you. This leper was living with an ailment, which causes perpetual psychological storms in its victim. His life was a continuous storm until He came across the Prince of Peace.

> *For to us a child is born, to us a son is given, and the government will be on his shoulders. And he will be called Wonderful Counselor, Mighty God, Everlasting Father, Prince of Peace. (Isaiah 9:6)*

In Mark 4:35-41, the Bible recounts how Jesus and His disciples were in a boat, buffeted by the storm. Jesus sentenced the storm to silence and then, there was peace. No matter the kind of "storm" in your life, just a brief encounter with Jesus Christ creates peace that endures.

DESPISED AND REJECTED

This leper was also a total reject. Both the society and his family rejected him. He was even rejected by the church. The day he met Jesus Christ, he met the compassion that willingly receives the forsaken. The psalmist tells us that the Lord will always receive us.

> *Though my father and mother forsake me, the LORD will receive me. (Psalm 27:10)*

If you are already born-again and you are sorrowful, it is because you have refused to claim your joy. If you are poor, it is because you refuse to claim your prosperity. If you are still in bondage, it is because you want to be in bondage. Your liberty in Christ is waiting.

BUT FOR JESUS ...

Who is this "only begotten Son" that was given to us? He is called Emmanuel, which means, "God with us".

> *Therefore the Lord himself will give you a sign: The virgin will be with child and will give birth to a son, and will call him Immanuel. (Isaiah 7:14)*

What does this imply? If God had not been with us, the result would have been disaster. If God the Father had not given us God the Son, where would we have been? If His blood – which cleanses from all sins – had not been shed for us, where would we end up?

> *If anyone's name was not found written in the book of life, he was thrown into the lake of fire.*
> *(Revelation 20: 15)*

The lake of fire had been lounging there, longingly waiting to barbecue us, but for this gift – Jesus – who changed that deadly destiny. If a trace of sin remains in one's life when he or she dies, such a fellow is heading, full steam, for hell-fire.

If Emmanuel had not received those stripes that healed us (1 Peter 2:24), what would we have done when doctors and drugs became scarce commodities – like it so often happens in some less privileged parts of the world? Thank God for His stripes. What would we have done if there was no Holy Spirit to quicken our mortal bodies (Romans 8:11)?

According to Romans 8:37, we are more than conquerors because of God who loved us. And, according to Romans 8:31, if God is on our side, it is inconsequential who is against us. Many of us would have been dead by now had God not remained with us. There are those who hate you just because God loves you. There are those who hate you because God makes you prosper. Even if you have only one outfit to your name, there will be people who will hate you because it looks so good on you. The people who hate you the most might be the people you shake hands and share smiles with, every morning. However, because God is with you, they have not been able to destroy you.

THE ALPHA AND THE OMEGA

The Lord tells us more about the One given to us.

> 'I am the Alpha and the Omega, "says the Lord God,' 'who is, and who was, and who is to come, the Almighty."
> (Revelation 1:8)

He is the Controller of the past because He is Alpha, the beginning. He is the Controller of the future because He is the Omega, the end. When He forgives your sins He simply exercises His control over the present and prevailing issues. It is with the same authority that He guarantees the well-being of the righteous.

As Alpha, He holds the sole and supreme mandate to change someone – who qualifies for eternal damnation – into a brand new creature through His Son Jesus Christ. That's the assurance which fuels our faith when we affirm that we have a great future. Philippians 4:4 states that we should rejoice in the Lord always. If our joy is not in Him, what kind of joy would we have in a world where change is the only constant? Our joy is in the Lord – Who does not change – therefore our joy can last forever.

Thank God for Emmanuel. Thank God for the Gift of God. Believers need to praise God and thank Him for this precious Gift – Jesus Christ – Whose blood cleansed away our sins, Whose body received the stripes that brought us healing. We need to thank God for the Holy Spirit that quickens our mortal bodies with joy that lasts forever, making us more than conquerors over countless enemies.

If you are not a believer, you are lost. Give your life to Him and you will experience a glorious change too great for the whole world to contain.

Chapter 1
Love Gives

For God so loved the world that he gave his one and only Son, that whoever believes in him shall not perish but have eternal life. (John 3:16)

This is a common Bible passage we often quote when talking to those outside our belief system. It conveys the need for them to respond to God's sacrificial love by submitting to the authority of Jesus Christ. We usually stress the need for them to avail themselves of God's promise of everlasting life. We remind them that God has no plans for them to perish but that rejecting Him automatically means eternal suicide. However, I have since discovered that there is a lot more than we normally consider.

As a matter of fact, the passage might not be as important to the sinner as it is to the saint. I have discovered a lot of blessings in the passage and I would like to share some of them. The first thing I discovered is that love gives. God so loved the world that He gave. You can never demonstrate love adequately without giving. My second discovery is that love gives the best. You can give to a beggar or a homeless guy roaming the streets without loving him. When you love someone, you give your best to that person. God gave His only begotten Son, the best He had.

Thirdly, love gives sacrificially. God made a supreme sacrifice by giving His only begotten Son to the world. If you study the Scriptures thoroughly, you will discover that God the Father and God the Son were never separated until the demands of the salvation plan pulled them apart – all because of you and I. God the Son carried our sins on the cross. Therefore, God the Father had to take His eyes away from the Son for three hours. From eternity past to eternity present, that separation would never have occurred. But, because of God's love for you and I, He made that sacrifice.

Love also gives willingly. God was not forced to give. Nobody compelled God to give us Jesus, yet He gave willingly because He wanted to give. Jesus Christ said:

> *Greater love has no one than this, that he lay down his life for his friends. (John 15:13)*

Jesus gave us His life as a sacrifice just as God gave Him to us, as His best, willingly and sacrificially. Jesus also gave His best, willingly.

> *The reason my Father loves me is that I lay down my life – only to take it up again. No one takes it from me, but I lay it down of my own accord I have authority to lay it down and authority to take it up again. This command I received from my Father. (John 10:17-18)*

PASSING THE TEST

Jesus is telling us here that nobody compelled Him to die. He did it of His own volition. He willingly laid down His life.

From the Scriptures, we see that from time to time, God demanded proof from those who claimed to love Him. God tested Abraham:

> *Some time later God tested Abraham. He said to him, "Abraham!" "Here I am," he replied. Then God said, "Take your son, your only son, Isaac, whom you love, and go to the region of Moriah. Sacrifice him there as a burnt offering on one of the mountains I will tell you about."*
> *(Genesis 22:1-2)*

The word "tempt" appears in the Kings James version of the Bible, but other translations have put it in perspective and it should read "test" as in the original Hebrew translation. Abraham was God's friend and he was put to the test. God wanted to know whether he would give, give his best, give sacrificially and give willingly. God told him to sacrifice his only son. Abraham did not argue. God told him to travel to the mount of Moriah, which was a three-day journey, to see whether or not Abraham would change his mind.

The devil must have tried to tempt Abraham to change his mind. However, Abraham did not falter. What may not be clear to the casual reader is that Abraham did not tell his wife that he was going to sacrifice Isaac. In fact, he did not tell Isaac himself. The fact that he told nobody, showed his determination to give.

Paul, once Saul of Tarsus, is a good example. He was very wicked; persecuting Christians was his goal in life. But God met him on his demonic mission to Damascus and saved his soul. Suddenly, Paul discovered that God loved him specifically. In fact, he uncovered the eternal truth of how long God had loved him – from his mother's womb – just as He has loved you from your mother's womb.

There is no doubt about this because you could have died while in the womb. You could have been a still-born child. The evil realm knew when your mother conceived and could have done something about it. When you were born, the forces of darkness could forecast your great future. That could have spurred a satanic sentence against your life but God, Who loved you so much, kept you from coming to any harm.

WHAT ARE YOU WILLING TO LAY ON THE LINE?

Once Paul realized that God loved him, he decided to reciprocate God's love. Paul was presented an opportunity to show his love for God when a prophecy challenged his plans to preach in Jerusalem. God sent word that he would suffer if he went to Jerusalem (Acts 21:4-14). Paul brushed this message aside – even when it was confirmed by a prophet. Paul was adamant about publicly confessing his faith in Jerusalem, at the risk of personal injury – even death. He was ready for anything. He said he was ready to die for Jesus Christ. That was what God wanted to find out.

From time to time, God will ask, "Do you love me?" When the answer is yes, He demands proof. If you say you love God, He may ask you to demonstrate it in one way or another. He may ask you to give – give your best, give sacrificially. And you must give willingly because God loves a cheerful giver. He may not ask for your money but may tax your time. He may ask for your talent. He may ask for your strength. He may ask for your entire life. He may call you into full-time ministry.

One beautiful thing is that love reciprocated reproduces greater love. In other words, if I demonstrate my love for you, unless you are the devil, the natural reaction is that you will love me more. If I smile at you, the natural reaction is for you to smile back at me. If you return my smile with a frown, you are either angry with me or you are demon possessed.

Each time you prove to God that you love Him, God responds with greater love for you. This is why Acts 20:35 blatantly declares that it is more blessed to give than to receive. When you are giving, you are actually opening the door to receive more. Because of God's eternal law of harvest, everyone who demonstrates love gets something better than they gave.

> *Do not be deceived: God cannot be mocked. A man reaps what he sows. (Galatians 6:7)*

The harvest is always greater than the seed sown. Because God gave His only begotten Son, He got many more sons into glory. He gave one Son and now He has millions of sons and daughters all over the world.

> *But we see Jesus, who was made a little lower than the angels, now crowned with glory and honor because he suffered death, so that by the grace of God he might taste death for everyone. In bringing many sons to glory, it was fitting that God, for whom and through whom everything exists, should make the author of their salvation perfect through suffering. (Hebrews 2:9-10)*

The Bible tells us that because Jesus Christ gave His life, God has exalted Him and has given him a Name that is above every other name so that at the name of Jesus, every knee should bow.

> *And being found in appearance as a man, he humbled himself and became obedient to death – even death on a cross! Therefore God exalted him to the highest place and gave him the name that is above every name, that at the name of Jesus every knee should bow, in heaven and on earth and under the earth, and every tongue confess that Jesus Christ is Lord, to the glory of God the Father.*
> *(Philippians 2:8-11)*

THE REWARD OF THE RIGHTEOUS

What happened after Abraham proved his love to God?

> *The angel of the LORD called to Abraham from heaven a second time and said, "I swear by myself, declares the LORD, that because you have done this and have not withheld your son, your only son, I will surely bless*

> *you and make your descendants as numerous as the stars in the sky and as the sand on the seashore. Your descendants will take possession of the cities of their enemies, and through your offspring all nations on earth will be blessed, because you have obeyed me.*
> *(Genesis 22:15-18)*

God swore that He would so bless Abraham that the blessings will spill over to the whole world. When it becomes possible to count the sands on the seashore, then it will be possible to hold a census of Abraham's descendants. All over the world today, are people – not even Jews – who are seeds of Abraham by the spiritual symbiosis of Abraham and God's labors of love.

God went on to say that no enemy would be able to overcome his seed. Because you are of the seed of Abraham, there is no way that the enemy can overcome you. They can try but they will not succeed.

> *God did extraordinary miracles through Paul, so that even handkerchiefs and aprons that had touched him were taken to the sick, and their illnesses were cured and the evil spirits left them. (Acts 19:11-12)*

Why did God do these extraordinary miracles? Because Paul loved God so much that he was willing to lay down his life. He demonstrated his love for God. The result: while Paul was still here on earth, God showed him the crown that he would wear in Heaven:

> *I have fought the good fight, I have finished the race, I have kept the faith. Now there is in store for me the crown of righteousness, which the Lord, the righteous judge, will award to me on that day – and not only to me, but also to all who have longed for his appearing.*
> *(2 Timothy 4:7-8)*

Solomon demonstrated his love for God by giving a thousand offerings. Then, God asked Solomon to make his request. Solomon asked for wisdom and God gave him wisdom and other things for which he did not ask. I am sure that there are some things I should have asked for that I did not even know to ask for. I know that the demonstration of my love for God will bring me more blessing than I can think to ask Him for.

I do not know about you, but I know that I love God. I love Him because He first loved me. Do you love God? Do you love Jesus Christ? Have you been struggling with yourself and rejecting His love? If you reject His love, you may be inviting His wrath. His love is sweeter than anything else. Give your life to Jesus Christ and He will wash you in His blood and demonstrate His love for you. If you are already born-again, tell Him that you want to love Him more. Tell Him to give you the grace to demonstrate your love for Him.

Chapter 2
Love Gives Life

God loved us and He gave us a Gift. We will now look at the significance of this Gift on different grounds. This Gift is the Gift of life. In fact, Jesus Christ said in John 14:6 that He is the Way, the Truth and the Life. Jesus Christ also said in John 10:10 that He has come that we might have life and have it more abundantly.

What then is life? It is easy to define life as the opposite of death. Death is permanent separation from things, people and places. Jesus Christ was given to us so that we will not die.

> *Jesus said to her, 'I am the resurrection and the life. He who believes in me will live, even though he dies."*
> *(John 11:25)*

> *And if the Spirit of him who raised Jesus from the dead is living in you, he who raised Christ from the dead will*

> *also give life to your mortal bodies through his Spirit, who lives in you. (Romans 8:11)*

Jesus Christ was given to us so that we will not die, financially. To be financially dead means to be bankrupt. If you are dead financially, Jesus will raise you up:

> *For you know the grace of our Lord Jesus Christ, that though he was rich, yet for your sakes he became poor, so that you through his poverty might become rich.*
> *(2 Corinthians 8:9)*

He became poor so that we might become rich. Also, Psalm 23:1 says because He, is our Shepherd, we will enjoy sufficiency. Psalm 34:10 says those who seek the Lord will not lack anything good. Philippians 4:19 says the Lord will meet all our needs through Christ Jesus.

He was also given to us so that we might not die mentally. A man who is mentally dead is a man who has lost his mind. The Bible tells us in 2 Timothy 1:7 that the Almighty God has given us sound minds. In John 14:27, Jesus Christ said He has given us peace which surpasses the world's understanding. In John 16:24 He encourages us to ask until our joy is full.

He was given to us so that we will not be dead spiritually.

Spiritual death means separation from God. When Adam sinned, humanity was separated from God. Initially, the first man, Adam, enjoyed intimate fellowship with God before sin showed up on the scene to separate him from God. Jesus Christ came that we might be re-united with God and never again to be separated from Him.

> *"Do not let your hearts be troubled. Trust in God; trust also in me. In my Father's house are many rooms; if it were not so, I would have told you. I am going there to prepare a place for you. And if I go and prepare a place for you, I will come back and take you to be with me that you also may be where I am." (John 14:1-3)*

If you belong to the Lord Jesus Christ, there is a place reserved for you in God's house, where you will live forever. In the meantime, John 14:16-17 says we are in close contact with God through God the Holy Spirit. Jesus was given to us so that we can have a permanent relationship with Almighty God all the days of our lives.

How has it become possible for us to live physically, live financially, live mentally and to live spiritually? Jesus Christ has come to save us from our sins through His blood.

> *But if we walk in the light, as he is in the light, we have fellowship with one another, and the blood of Jesus, his Son, purifies us from all sin. (1 John 1:7)*

When He cleanses us from all our sins, He transforms us, and we become brand new creatures.

> *Therefore, if anyone is in Christ, he is a new creation; the old has gone, the new has come! (2 Corinthians 5:17)*

Not only will He forgive our sins, if we will allow Him to, He will break the power of sin over us.

> *For sin shall not be your master, because you are not under law, but under grace. (Romans 6:14)*

If you are not living the way God wants you to live – enjoying physical, financial and mental health – you have no joy and you have lost contact with the Holy Spirit. The cause may also be that you refused to let go of sin.

> *For if you live according to the sinful nature, you will die; but if by the Spirit you put to death the misdeeds of the body, you will live. (Romans 8:13)*

If you allow the flesh to win you over and you yield to temptation – in spite of the fact that Jesus Christ was given to you to give you life – you will die. You must let go of sin. We cannot continue in sin and expect grace to abound.

LIFE MORE ABUNDANTLY

There are some of us who already have life. By the grace of God, we are living holy, and we are healthy in all spheres of life. What about abundant life? No matter how well it is with you now, it can be better.

> *Forget the former things; do not dwell on the past. See, I am doing a new thing! Now it springs up; do you not perceive it? I am making a way in the desert and streams in the wasteland. (Isaiah 43:18-19)*

He will do a new thing. No matter how wonderful life is with you today, God is willing to take you to greater heights.

> *However, as it is written: "No eye has seen, no ear has heard, no mind has conceived what God has prepared for those who love him" but God has revealed it to us by his Spirit. The Spirit searches all things, even the deep things of God. (1 Corinthians 2:9-10)*

Anything that you have seen already is worse than what is yet to come. If you want abundant life, you need to understand that real life comes from service. Those who would enjoy abundant life must learn to serve others. The Lord said that the one who wants to be the greatest should be the servant of all. Life is only meaningful when you are serving others.

> *Then the mother of Zebedee's sons came to Jesus with her sons and, kneeling down, asked a favor of him. "What is it you want?" he asked She said, "Grant that one of these two sons of mine may sit at your right and the other at your left in your kingdom." "You don't know what you are asking," Jesus said to them. "Can you drink the cup I am going to drink?" "We can," they answered. Jesus said to them, "You will indeed drink from my cup, but to sit at my right or left is not for me to grant. These places belong to those for whom they have been prepared by my Father." When the ten heard about this, they were indignant with the two brothers. Jesus called them together and said, "You know that the rulers of the Gentiles lord it over them,*

> *and their high officials exercise authority over them. Not so with you. Instead, whoever wants to become great among you must be your servant, and whoever wants to be first must be your slave – just as the Son of Man did not come to be served, but to serve, and to give his life as a ransom for many. (Matthew 20:20-28)*

Jesus Christ, Himself, said that it is more blessed to give than to receive.

> *In everything I did, I showed you that by this kind of hard work we must help the weak, remembering the words the Lord Jesus himself said: 'It is more blessed to give than to receive. (Acts 20:35)*

Abundant life is in giving and serving. Abundant life is in having a life that is of use to others. Let your life be meaningful.

> *The thief comes only to steal and kill and destroy; I have come that they may have life, and have it to the full*
> *(John 10:10)*

This passage opens our eyes again to a great secret – why Jesus came into the world. According to this Bible passage, there is life; there is abundant life and then there is more abundant life. When we talk about life, automatically, we talk about death because the two of them go together. Death means the absence of life. Life means the absence of death.

THE LIVING DEAD

The Bible tells us that spiritually, we were dead in trespasses and sin (Ephesians 2:1), until Jesus Christ came and He quickened or made us alive. Any unbeliever is as good as dead.

There are many dead, who are yet breathing. They are the living dead. A very good example is the story of the leper found in Matthew 8:1-3. In the Bible days, a leper was as good as dead. He had to live in seclusion, outside the city or in the bush. The moment the leper in this text got in contact with Jesus Christ, his status changed from a living dead to life.

The woman with the issue of blood, in Mark 5:25-34, was also as the living dead. But, when she grabbed a hold on to Jesus' garment, death departed from her and she received virtue from the fountain of life.

Bartimeaus was blind and was as the living dead before he met Jesus Christ. Then, all of a sudden, his eyes became open; he threw away the ungainly garment of sorrow he had on and he never begged again.

Jesus wants us to have abundant life. An example of abundant life is that of David.

> *So he asked Jesse, are these all the sons you have?" "There is still the youngest," Jesse answered, "but he is tending the sheep." Samuel said, "Send for him; we will not sit down until he arrives." So he sent and had him brought in. He was ruddy, with a fine appearance and handsome features. Then the LORD said, "Rise and anoint him; he is the one." So Samuel took the horn of oil and anointed him in the presence of his brothers, and from that day on the Spirit of the LORD came upon David in power. Samuel then went to Ramah. (1 Samuel 16:11-13)*

David was a shepherd boy, alive physically and spiritually. He was promoted from shepherd boy to king.

The life of abundance is the plan of God for our lives. God wants to make kings and queens of many who are still living their lives as messengers. There are many who are just struggling to survive. We find a very classical example in 2 Samuel:

> *When Mephibosheth son of Jonathan, the son of Saul came to David, he bowed down to pay him honor. David said, "Mepbiboshetb!" "Your servant," he replied. "Don't be afraid," David said to him, "for I will surely show you kindness for the sake of your father Jonathan.*

> *I will restore to you all the land that belonged to your grandfather Saul and you will always eat at my table." Mephibosheth bowed down and said, "What is your servant, that you should notice a dead dog like me?"*
> *(2 Samuel 9:6-8)*

Mephibosheth was a prince by inheritance. However, because he was lame, he lived the life of a slave. That is until David came to his rescue. One of the major reasons that some of us are like Mephibosheth is because of wrong teachings. Some of us have been taught – and we have accepted the teaching – that if we are to make Heaven, we must be poor. Do you not know that Jesus Christ became poor that we might become rich?

The beauty of the sacrificial love of God and its significance in our lives is that you can go from death to life, to abundant life and then to life more abundant, in just one day. There is an example found in the story of Esther. She was a slave. Her life was as good as dead. The Almighty God caused Mordecai, her uncle, to love her so much that he adopted her. It was not long after that the Almighty God promoted her to the position of a queen. She moved a step further and became the deliverer of a whole nation.

LOVE GIVES EVERLASTING LIFE

What exactly is everlasting life? This means life that lasts forever. What is real life? A look at this Scripture might help us understand what life is all about.

> *And he told them this parable: "The ground of a certain rich man produced a good crop. He thought to himself, 'What shall I do? I have no place to store my crops.' Then he said, "This is what I'll do. I will tear down my barns and build bigger ones, and there I will store all my grain and my goods. And I'll say to myself, "You have plenty of good things laid up for many years. Take life easy; eat, drink and be merry." "But God said to him," You fool! This very*

> *night your life will be demanded from you. Then who will get what you have prepared for yourself" (Luke 12:16-20)*

Here, the Bible tells of a man whose agricultural investment was excellently rewarded. He said he would build bigger barns to hoard his produce. Then, he would just sit back and sink in into a life of revelry – wining and dining. The Bible said God called him a fool and demanded his soul – he died.

In Luke 12:15, Jesus Christ said that the life of a man does not consist in the abundance of his possessions. Life is not in wealth, or how much you acquire. Life is not in beauty because Proverbs 31:30 tells us that beauty is transient. Jesus Christ said in John 6:63 that the flesh is inconsequential. Real beauty is a product of salvation because God said He would beautify the meek with salvation. 2 Kings 5:1 reminds us of Naaman who was great and powerful but he was a leper.

Life is not in power plays. Power belongs to God. Power is a passing thing. Life is not in great achievements. As soon as Nebuchadnezzar finished his infamous statement, boasting about his area of jurisdiction and influence, God cut him down to the grass-eating status for seven years. (Daniel 4:29-33)

WHAT LIFE REALLY IS

Life is not in education or worldly wisdom; otherwise, Solomon, the wisest man who ever lived, would not have said that everything is vanity. What really is life?

> *Now this is eternal life: that they may know you, the only true God, and Jesus Christ, whom you have sent.*
> *(John 17:3)*

Life is lived to know God and Jesus Christ.

> *This is what the LORD says: "Let not the wise man boast of his wisdom or the strong man boast of his strength or the rich man boast of his riches, but let him who boasts boast about this: that he understands and knows me,*

> *that I am the LORD, who exercises kindness, justice and righteousness on earth, for in these I delight, " declares the LORD. (Jeremiah 9:23-24)*

You should glory in the fact that you know God. Knowing God is having eternal life. Knowing God brings about miracles.

> *Those who do wickedly against the covenant he shall corrupt with flattery; but the people who know their God shall be strong, and carry out great exploits.*
> *(Daniel 11:32 NKJV)*

What type of exploits are we talking about here? Jesus Christ talked about certain exploits.

> *And these signs will accompany those who believe: In my name they will drive out demons; they will speak in new tongues; they will pick up snakes with their hands; and when they drink deadly poison, it will not hurt them at all; they will place their hands on sick people, and they will get well. (Mark 16:17-18)*

When you lay hands on a blind man and he can see, you will know that that's what life means. When you pray for the barren and she conceives, you will know this is what life should be and who God is. When your life begins to bring joy to other lives, this is life. When people get blessed wherever you go, you know this is what life should be.

You can realize this joy-giving life by simply believing in the Almighty God, Who so loved the world that He gave His only begotten Son for you to love in return. If only you can believe in Him, you will be able to cast out demons, challenge the devil, heal the sick and your life will become a blessing to others.

If you have given your life to Jesus Christ, it can only mean that you know God. If you do not know God, you cannot accept His Son. Life is about getting to know God. If you are yet to know Him, you can start today. Submit to His authority now and He will give you eternal life from hereon.

Chapter 3
Love Bestows Blessings

He who did not spare his own Son, but gave him up for us all - how will he not also, along with him, graciously give us all things? (Romans 8:32)

When you look at all the blessings that came through the fact that God gave us His only begotten Son, you will be amazed. For example, the blood of Jesus Christ cleanses us from all sins.

But if we walk in the light, as he is in the light, we have fellowship with one another, and the blood of Jesus, his Son, purifies us from all sin. (1 John 1:7)

Because God gave us Jesus Christ, who paid for all our sins with His blood, we can now be free from all our sins.

Therefore, there is now no condemnation for those who are in Christ Jesus, because through Christ Jesus the law

> *of the Spirit of life set me free from the law of sin and death. (Romans 8:1-2)*

Because God gave us His Son, we can now say with all boldness, that there is no condemnation for us. In other words, if the devil comes around to remind you – as he has often tried me – of some sins you committed before you became a believer, all you have to tell him is that there is no condemnation for you now because you are in Christ Jesus.

> *In all these things we are more than conquerors through him who loved us. (Romans 8:37)*

We are more than conquerors not because we know how to pray or because we know how to live holy, but simply because of Him (God) Who loved us. Because God gave us Jesus Christ, we are guaranteed victory.

THE AUTHORITY OF THE BELIEVER

We have victory in every sphere of life:

> *Therefore God exalted him to the highest place and gave him the name that is above every name, that at the name of Jesus every knee should bow, in heaven and on earth and under the earth, and every tongue confess that Jesus Christ is Lord, to the glory of God the Father.*
> *(Philippians 2:9-11)*

This implies that because God gave us His only begotten Son, we know that when sickness comes, we can tell sickness to bow out of our lives, at the name of Jesus. When demons try to oppress, we command them to bow at the name of Jesus. When problems come, we tell them to bow at the name of Jesus. If they do not want to bow willingly, we have been given the authority to enforce our mandate and they must bow.

> *And these signs will accompany those who believe: In my name they will drive out demons; they will speak in new*

> *tongues; they will pick up snakes with their hands; and when they drink deadly poison, it will not hurt them at all; they will place their hands on sick people, and they will get well. (Mark 16:17-18)*

We have been given the authority to compel them to bow. Why? Because… in the name of Jesus, we shall cast out demons, according to the Word of God. God gave us His best, so now we have the authority to command demons.

However, love is a two-way street. If I love you and you do not love me in return, very soon, my love will grow cold. The Almighty God is no exception. If you search the Scriptures, you will discover that for everything He does for you, He expects something in return. For example, in Philippians 4:19 it is written that God will supply all our needs according to His riches in glory by Christ Jesus. All our needs are already supplied in that single gift.

WHAT DOES GOD NEED FROM US?

God has needs too – two needs – and He wants us to satisfy them. The first need is recorded in Isaiah:

> *Then I heard the voice of the Lord saying, "Whom shall I send? And who will go for us?" And I said, "Here am I. Send me!" (Isaiah 6:8)*

Thousands of years ago, Isaiah heard the all-important question. God is still asking that question even today. He needs ambassadors who will go everywhere as His representatives.

The second need is written in John:

> *Yet a time is coming and has now come when the true worshipers will worship the Father in spirit and truth, for they are the kind of worshipers the Father seeks. God is spirit, and his worshipers must worship in spirit and in truth. (John 4:23-24)*

> *I baptize you with water for repentance. But after me will come one who is more powerful than I, whose sandals I am not fit to carry. He will baptize you with the Holy Spirit and with fire. (Matthew 3:11)*

This Bible passage explains how we will be baptized with the Holy Ghost and fire. In other words, God will make sure that the Holy Ghost will anoint us with tremendous power so that we will be able to glorify Him, as we ought. We cannot glorify God unaided but by the help of the Holy Spirit.

> *But when he, the Spirit of truth, comes, he will guide you into all truth. He will not speak on his own; he will speak only what he hears, and he will tell you what is yet to come. He will bring glory to me by taking from what is mine and making it known to you. (John 16:13-14)*

> *But you will receive power when the Holy Spirit comes on you; and you will be my witnesses in Jerusalem, and in all Judea and Samaria, and to the ends of the earth.*
> *(Acts 1:8)*

As soon as you are determined to be His ambassador, He will supply the power through the Holy Spirit.

> *And from Jesus Christ, who is the faithful witness, the firstborn from the dead, and the ruler of the kings of the earth. To him who loves us and has freed us from our sins by his blood, and has made us to be a kingdom and priests to serve his God and Father - to him be glory and power for ever and ever! Amen. (Revelation 1:5-6)*

This text tells us that He will make us priests and kings. The moment you accept the Lord Jesus Christ, God says He will transform you from an ordinary person to a priest and king. He will do this because He wants something in return.

> *But you are a chosen people, a royal priesthood, a holy nation, a people belonging to God, that you may declare*

> *the praises of him who called you out of darkness into his wonderful light. (1 Peter 2:9)*

He will make us priests and kings so that we will spend the rest of our lives praising Him. When He makes you a king and a priest, you are to show forth His praise.

YOUR SUCCESS GLORIFIES GOD

The Bible states that we can do all things through Christ who strengthens us. The same gift from God ensures that you become an achiever. An achiever is someone who always succeeds. There is no failure for someone who has the support of Jesus Christ. I am challenging you to think big and hook your faith to the Word of God:

> *I can do everything through him who gives me strength. (Philippians 4:13)*

This is, however, subject to one condition:

> *So whether you eat or drink or whatever you do, do it all for the glory of God. (1 Corinthians 10:31)*

You should do everything to the glory of God. If your purpose is to glorify yourself, you have failed before you even started. God will only supply the strength if you are willing to glorify Him.

Jesus Christ made this promise:

> *You may ask me for anything in my name, and I will do it. (John 14:14)*

The first time I read this passage, I paused to ponder over it.

As a mathematician, to me, "all" means "without exception". Anyone, who says he can do everything you ask him to, is either crazy or is the Almighty. Just then I remembered that in John 14:6, Jesus Christ said He is the Way, the Truth and the Life. If He is the Truth, it means that He can never lie. I remember that on that day, I told God to heal me from incessant malaria attacks. I promised that in return, I would serve Him for the rest of my life.

He will do whatever you want but you must keep His commandments.

> *If you love me, you will obey what I command.*
> *(John 14:15)*

You must do whatever He wants. I believe this is a very fair bargain. How much does He want from you? Very little. How much do you want from Him? A lot. I want a lot from God. I am always asking for one thing or another from Him.

MAKING GOD SMILE

The story of an Indian, who became born again and decided that he would make God happy, should shed some more light on what we need to really understand. I think he dreamed that he presented his blanket as a gift to God and he wanted God to smile to show that He was happy. God did not smile. He went back and gave his precious horse to God. God did not smile. He then presented his bow and arrow, which were his means of livelihood. Yet, God did not smile. Finally, he came to God and said, "Indian brought blanket, Indian brought horse, Indian brought bow and arrow, now Indian has brought Indian." It was then that God smiled.

In summary, God wants you. Because He gave Himself for you, He wants you to give yourself to Him. You should be willing to do so. Once He owns you, He owns whatever you have. Once you submit to His authority, it becomes very easy to do whatever He asks. The moment you are willing to do whatever He asks, the joy in it is that whatever you ask of Him, He will do.

CHAPTER 4
LOVE FUELS FRIENDSHIP

If God loves the world, that means He loves Nigeria, America – you name the country. It means that God loves my village and your birthplace. This also means that God loves my family and God loves me. If the world were to shrink down to only one person, just you, then "God so loved the world" would mean, "God so loved you". God's love for us is so real that He gave His only begotten Son, that if we believe in Him, we will not perish but have everlasting life. That means that we are very important people. I am so important that Jesus died for me. You may not agree with this fact but God agrees.

There is only one friend in the whole world. Every other fellow is a brother, a sister or an absolute enemy. The only friend is JESUS.

The best story on friendship recorded in the Bible was the heart-lock between Jonathan and David. Their friendship never ceases to bring tears to the eyes of many. Let's look at it:

> *After David had finished talking with Saul Jonathan became one in spirit with David, and he loved him as himself. From that day Saul kept David with him and did not let him return to his father's house. And Jonathan made a covenant with David because he loved him as himself Jonathan took off the robe he was wearing and gave it to David, along with his tunic, and even his sword, his bow and his belt. (I Samuel 18:1-4)*

Jonathan loved David like his own soul and he began to do what we have already learned that love does. Love gives, so Jonathan began to give. He gave David his robe, his belt and jacket, and his sword. You will want to call this true friendship. However, if you study this relationship, you will find out that it was very imperfect. There was something Jonathan could have given David, which he did not give him. He could have given him his shoes. The Bible tells us why shoes are important.

> *Now in earlier times in Israel for the redemption and transfer of property to become final, one party took off his sandal and gave it to the other. This was the method of legalizing transactions in Israel. (Ruth 4:7)*

In those days, an agreement was not complete until the shoes were given in addition. Because Jonathan did not give his shoes, it meant that he could retrieve all that he gave David at any time in the future. Also in those days, servants never wore shoes. Only the children wore shoes. The popular Sunday school story of the prodigal son illustrates this (Luke 15:17-24).

The prodigal son demanded his portion of the heirloom, ran away from home and squandered his inheritance. When he became broke, he accepted menial jobs including working on a pig farm. The moment he became a servant, he lost the privilege of wearing shoes. He repented and went back home. On his return, his father saw him afar and received him with gladness.

He told his servants to dress him up, put a ring on his hand and shoes on his feet.

> *But the father said to his servants, 'Quick! Bring the best robe and put it on him. Put a ring on his finger and sandals on his feet. (Luke 15:22)*

His sonship was restored when his father gave him shoes. Jonathan did not give David his shoes. Inadvertently, he was saying that even though they were friends, David must recognize his status and remember that he is a servant. In addition, each time Jonathan visited David – the fugitive – David would continue his hibernation in the bush while Jonathan would return to the palace.

> *After the boy had gone, David got up from the south side [of the stone} and bowed down before Jonathan three times, with his face to the ground. Then they kissed each other and wept together - but David wept the most. Jonathan said to David, "Go in peace, for we have sworn friendship with each other in the name of the LORD, saying, 'The LORD is witness between you and me, and between your descendants and my descendants forever.'" Then David left, and Jonathan went back to the town. (1 Samuel 20:41-42)*

I thought that a friend in need must be a friend indeed. The most frightening thing is that all the while that Jonathan was demonstrating this love to David, he had a hidden agenda. Somehow, God had revealed something to both Saul and Jonathan.

> *And Saul's son Jonathan went to David at Horesh and helped him find strength in God. "Don't be afraid. " he said. "My father Saul will not lay a hand on you. You will be king over Israel and I will be second to you. Even my father Saul knows this." The two of them made a covenant before the LORD. Then Jonathan went home, but David remained at Horesh. (1 Samuel 23:16-18)*

Jonathan knew that God's will was for David to be the next king of Israel. He said he would be content to be David's assistant. This shows that all the while that he was giving, he had an agenda. When somebody makes you his best friend, there's usually a hidden agenda somewhere.

But Jesus loves you and I, perfectly. At the climax of His life, which was ultimately sacrificed for us, one of the first things He gave was His pair of shoes. No one is crucified with shoes on. He surrendered His shoes freely.

> He came to that which was his own, but his own did not receive him. Yet to all who received him, to those who believed in his name, he gave the right to become children of God. (John 1:11-12)

The moment God met you and I, He made us sons.

> How great is the love the Father has lavished on us, that we should be called children of God! And that is what we are! The reason the world does not know us is that it did not know him. (1 John 3:1)

Jesus called us sons. Jesus will never leave us or forsake us – not even for a moment – like Jonathan left David. Even if we are passing through fire, He will walk with us. Even in deep waters, He will be there with us. When we are walking through the valley of the shadow of death, He will be there with us. He even said if our parents forsake us, He will receive us. You may say but He is not here right now. But He is. He is always in the midst of two or three people gathered in His name. He went to Heaven to prepare a place for us.

> Do not let your hearts be troubled. Trust in God; trust also in me. In my Father's house are many rooms; if it were not so, I would have told you. I am going there to prepare a place for you. And if I go and prepare a place for you, I will come back and take you to be with me that you also may be where I am. (John 14:1-3)

When He finishes preparing the place, He will not send an angel for us. He will come Himself. Together, hand in hand, He will walk us to Heaven. I know that I have a friend. His name is JESUS. He loves me completely. He has no hidden agenda. He's with me anywhere I go. I can talk to Him anywhere. Anytime I need help, He will always be there, no matter the danger. Jesus is my friend. He is precious to me. I will keep on praising Him forever.

Chapter 5
Love Lends Heritage

God's immeasurable love for you and I cost Him His only begotten son, Jesus Christ. The love of God has benefits. One of which is that we can become children of God.

> *Yet to all who received him, to those who believed in his name, he gave the right to become children of God.*
> *(John 1:12)*

If you receive Jesus Christ, you can call yourself a child of God, without any doubt. Each lineage has its own automatic constants. For example, the blood of your father flows in your veins. There is a link between the blood of a father and the blood of his son. In much the same way, the blood of Almighty God, the Father, begins to flow in your veins once you become a believer. Jesus Christ said He is the Vine, and we are the branches:

> *I am the true vine, and my Father is the gardener. He cuts off every branch in me that bears no fruit, while every branch that does bear fruit he prunes so that it will be even more fruitful. (John 15:1-2)*

The same liquid that flows through the vine, flows through the branches. Whether you believe it or not, from the day you become born again, you undergo a divine blood transfusion. This is why witchcraft, the occult and any weapon from your adversary – which prey on blood-can never affect you.

THE NATURE OF GOD

The Bible confirms that we are partakers of the very nature of God.

> *Grace and peace be yours in abundance through the knowledge of God and of Jesus our Lord. His divine power has given us everything we need for life and godliness through our knowledge of him who called us by his own glory and goodness. Through these he has given us his very great and precious promises, so that through them you may participate in the divine nature and escape the corruption in the world caused by evil desires.*
> *(2 Peter 1:2-4)*

The very nature of God becomes available to you, the moment you become born again. Your nature becomes the same as that of God. As a result, God expects you to live a godly life. You are to live with power because He is an omnipotent God. He is the Lord God Almighty and He expects you, His child, to live a life which parades His power.

> *And these signs will accompany those who believe: In my name they will drive out demons; they will speak in new tongues; they will pick up snakes with their hands; and when they drink deadly poison, it will not hurt them at all; they will place their hands on sick people, and they will get well. (Mark 16:17-18)*

The moment you become born-again, your prayer life should change. You do not go about begging and crawling on the floor before you get anything from God. As a matter of fact, the Bible states that once you are a child of God, you are to rule by decrees. You are to cast out demons. You are also to speak in new tongues. You are to take up serpents; that is, you are to challenge the devil. If you drink any deadly thing, it won't hurt you because you have the blood of God in you. You are expected to lay hands on the sick and they will recover because your Father is the Healer.

As a child of God, you are also to rule with authority.

> *See, it is I who created the blacksmith who fans the coals into flame and forges a weapon fit for its work. And it is I who have created the destroyer to work havoc; no weapon forged against you will prevail, and you will refute every tongue that accuses you. This is the heritage of the servants of the LORD, and this is their vindication from me," declares the LORD. (Isaiah 54:16-17)*

He created the magical charms, witches and wizards, but He is assuring you that anything they put together against you will not function, once you are His child. He commands them not to function. Daniel's ordeal in the lion's den is a good illustration. God created lions to be flesh-eating animals but they could not eat Daniel up because God made sure they couldn't.

SUPERIOR TO THE NATURAL

He also says you are to condemn every tongue that rises against you in judgment. You are a prince of the Most High God. If anybody or any demon rises up against you, you are to condemn them with His authority. God expects that your conduct should be supernatural – superior to the natural. Your behavior should be different from that of other people because you are no longer "normal" but a child of God.

In truth, children of God perceive a certain peace, which is not normal, it is beyond this world. You will see, in a true believer, a certain confidence that the world cannot comprehend. While other people are afraid, the true believer remains calm; and people see them as abnormal. Definitely, children of God are not "normal" because of their peculiarities. It is because of these peculiarities that God wants us to be absolutely perfect. This may seem too difficult. In fact, once I took God up on this issue and He gave me an example. He said imagine clean water in a tiny reservoir, then imagine that a tiny piece of human waste mistakenly gets into the water, would it still be clean water?

> *To this you were called, because Christ suffered for you, leaving you an example, that you should fallow in his steps. He committed no sin, and no deceit was found in his mouth. (1 Peter 2:21-22)*

There was no guile found in Him as a result, there should be no guile found in you. For,

> *Whoever would love life and see good days must keep his tongue from evil and his lips from deceitful speech.*
> *(1 Peter 3:10)*

> *God is not a man, that he should lie, nor a son of man, that he should change his mind. Does he speak and then not act? Does he promise and not fulfill?*
> *(Numbers 23:19)*

God never lies.

James tells us what God expects from us:

> *Above all, my brothers, do not swear – not by heaven or by earth or by anything else. Let your "Yes" be yes, and your "No," no, or you will be condemned. (James 5:12)*

You are not allowed to tell lies, whatever the "color". God will not take half-truths. Your yes must be yes, and your no must be no. Everything that you do must be straightforward because He is straightforward and you are His child.

The promises of God are not yes and no but yes and amen.

> *For the Son of God, Jesus Christ, who was preached among you by me and Silas and Timothy, was not "Yes" and "No, " but in him it has always been "Yes." For no matter how many promises God has made, they are "Yes" in Christ. And so through him the "Amen" is spoken by us to the glory of God. (2 Corinthians 1:19-20)*

This means that once He has spoken, it is settled.

> *Every good and perfect gift is from above, coming down from the Father of the heavenly lights, who does not change like shifting shadows. (James 1:17)*

KEEP YOUR WORD

God is absolutely plain and completely constant. Therefore, you know where you stand with Him. When He makes a promise, you can go to bed without any doubt that the promise will be fulfilled. If you are going to be blessed by God you must always fulfill your promises.

> *LORD, who may dwell in your sanctuary? who may live on your holy hill? He whose walk is blameless and who does what is righteous, who speaks the truth from his heart and has no slander on his tongue, who does his neighbor no wrong and casts no slur on his fellowman, who despises a vile man but honors those who fear the LORD, who keeps his oath even when it hurts.*
> *(Psalm 15:1-4)*

Make a mental note of what verse 4 says because that's the crux of the matter. If you make a promise and you later discover that the promise is likely to bring you some injury, you must not change it.

> *When you make a vow to God, do not delay in fulfilling it. He has no pleasure in fools; fulfill your vow.*
> *(Ecclesiastes 5:4)*

If you make a vow and you do not pay it, the Bible states that you are a fool. Once you have made a promise, you must fulfill it, if you are truly a child of God. You may want to rationalize why God cannot lie on the fact that He is not a man while you are just human. The perfect answer to this can be found in 2 Corinthians:

> *Therefore, if anyone is in Christ, he is a new creation; the old has gone, the new has come! (2 Corinthians 5:17)*

When you become born-again, you are re-created. You become a new creature. The second answer is found in Colossians:

> *Do not lie to each other, since you have taken off your old self with its practices and have put on the new self, which is being renewed in knowledge in the image of its Creator. (Colossians 3:9-10)*

LIVE LIKE HIM

The old man will have to go for the new man to come in.

God will create a new garment for you to put on. You may still say that this is difficult. May I tell you that the choice is yours. You can choose to either live like Christ or to live like a mere mortal. Before you decide, read this Scripture:

> *But now, this is what the LORD says - he who created you, O Jacob, he who formed you, O Israel: "Fear not, for I have redeemed you; I have summoned you by name; you are mine. When you pass through the waters, I will be with you; and when you pass through the rivers, they will not sweep over you. When you walk through the fire, you will not be burned; the flames will not set you ablaze. (Isaiah 43:1-2)*

God is simply saying here that if you live like Him, you can walk on water. You can ride on top of every raging sea of life's riddles that you come across. But, the choice is yours. You may also decide to live like a mere man and sink. If you live like God, you can walk in fire and. it will not burn you, like Shadrach, Meshach and Abednego. If you want to live like a man, every fire of life, as well as the fury of the enemy, will burn you because God has no commitment to or from you.

God loves you so much that He wants you to be like Him.

Make a choice today. Will you live supernaturally like Him or will you live limited like the people of the world?

Chapter 6
Love Fosters Freedom

If somebody loves you so much that he decides to lay down his life for you, I think it is only wise that you should find out who he is and why he loves you so much. If someone writes you, promising to shield you from any danger or death, I think you ought to meet the person and find out who he is and why he loves you so much. This is what Paul said about Jesus Christ:

> *But whatever was to my profit I now consider loss for the sake of Christ. What is more, I consider everything a loss compared to the surpassing greatness of knowing Christ Jesus my Lord, for whose sake I have lost all things. I consider them rubbish, that I may gain Christ and be found in him, not having a righteousness of my own that comes from the law, but that which is through faith in Christ - the righteousness that comes from God and is by faith. I want to know Christ and the power*

> *of his resurrection and the fellowship of sharing in his sufferings, becoming like him in his death.*
> *(Philippians 3:7-10)*

He said Jesus paid every price possible that he might know Him. That he might know somebody who loved him so much that He willingly gave His life for him. Who is Jesus Christ? Why did He come? Jesus Christ explains his Agenda:

> *The thief comes only to steal and kill and destroy; I have come that they may have life, and have it to the full.*
> *(John 10:10)*

I think you ought to want to know this person. He said He has come to silence the devil in your life. I think you should want to know the One who dedicated His life to restore all that the devil has stolen from you. He pledged that He would be ever ready to neutralize any power of destruction that the devil has. I think you should know Who left all His glory in Heaven to come to the earth, all for you – to give you life... everlasting life.

What did this same Jesus say?

> *Greater love has no one than this, that he lay down his life for his friends. (John 15:13)*

In another part of the Bible, He said, one could consider staking one's life for a good man. However, what do you think of a man who dies for his enemies? Remember, the Bible states that Jesus died for us while we were still sinners. He died for us while we were yet the enemies of God – while we were still strangers to God and while we were still doing everything contrary to the Word of God. While Jesus hung on the cross, after all the beating and the torture... after the crown of thorns and the mocking.

> *When he had received the drink, Jesus said, "It is finished." With that, he bowed his head and gave up his spirit.*
> *(John 19:30)*

When He said, "It is finished", which also means, "Oh! Bride". In other words, He wanted us to appreciate the premium price He paid for our souls. He was saying that because of you, He suffered all the pain. He was saying that He endured the beating so that by His stripes you might be healed. He was saying that He shed His blood so that your sins could be washed away. He was saying that He became thirsty so, that you will never thirst. He was saying that He died so you will never die. He was saying that even His Father had to reject Him – for three horrible hours – for you to belong in His Kingdom. I think you should get to know He Who died for you. I think you should get to know Who paid that kind of price for you.

So if the Son sets you, free, you will be free indeed.
(John 8:36)

THE HIGHEST BIDDER

Consider this illustration to gain a better understanding: Satan took us to the auction grounds to sell us. The first bidder was Sickness, who assured Satan that he would afflict us with a disease that would make us reel around between the doctors, sorcerers, or the occult without release. The intention, of course, is to keep us under the direct – or indirect – control of Satan. Satan liked the idea.

The second bidder was Death. Death conveyed to Satan that we might have a chance to escape once our eyes were opened. He said he would kill us, once and for all, and give our souls to Satan. Satan saw this as a better offer. The third bidder was Jesus Christ. Jesus told Satan that He wanted to buy us; intrigued, Satan asked for His offer. Jesus said Satan should let us go and take Him instead. Satan jumped at this offer.

Satan set us free and took Jesus. Jesus was sold to Death but Death could not handle Jesus. On the third day, He rose again.

Meanwhile, as soon as Jesus died, Satan wanted to repossess us but He couldn't. When Jesus resurrected, He confronted Satan with the blood – sealed deal and told him that we are free because He has set us free. Jesus can choose to do what He wants with what He has paid for. Yes! Jesus died and rose on the third day just to set us free. But why did He do this? Answer: He cares for us.

> *Cast all your anxiety on him because he cares for you.*
> *(1 Peter 5:7)*

This is why I think you should get to know the One Who cares this much for you.

Jesus Christ was clearly transparent when He said this:

> *For the Son of Man came to seek and to save what was lost. (Luke 19:10)*

I was lost and He found me. Glory be to God! He found me because He loved me so much that He gave His Son to seek me out and save my soul. If God's government was a democracy and He asked my friends whether I should be saved, I know how they would vote. Many of my friends used to say that they were happy going to Hell because they knew that was where most of their friends would be. I used to keep this company but Jesus sought me out. He was determined that I would not go to Hell. God loved me so much that His Son chased after me and saved my soul. I think you should know the One Who saved my soul. I think you would like to know the One Who loves me this much.

HIS LOVE CONSTRAINS ME

When somebody loves you this much, should you make Him sad? Should you disregard Him? I find that it is easy to offend those who do not like me. After all, without even offending them, they are already angry with me. However, when I offend somebody that I love very much, it is premium pain – an indescribable pain.

> *For Christ's love compels us, because we are convinced that one died for all and therefore all died. And he*

> *died for all, that those who live should no longer live for themselves but for him who died for them and was raised again. (2 Corinthians 5:14-15)*

There are many things I could do but will not do because of the love of Christ. Many times, the love of Christ has constrained me. Temptations will come, but I am able to say "no", because I do not want Jesus, Who loves me, to be unhappy. He loves me very much and I am not going to do anything that will make Him sad.

After one of my friends became born-again, he still had one little problem. He was a chain smoker. One day this "chimney" visited me. While we were talking, he said he would stop smoking if I can show him in the Bible where it is written that he should not smoke. I simply asked him that if he was sure that Jesus was living in him, does he think that Jesus would feel comfortable with all the soot he was forcing on Him? On his way home, he pondered what I said and searched himself to see whether there was anything he could not give up for the One Who loves him. He finally decided that if Jesus died for him, then he would stop smoking. That was the last time he smoked cigarettes. The love of God constrained him.

Why not join me in worshipping the One Who saved my soul... the One Who loved me so... the One Who is the King of kings and the Lord of lords... the One Who died for me and paid the price. He is the One Who set me free. He is the One Who cares for me. His name is JESUS.

Chapter 7
Love Bequeths Benefits

God so loved the world that He gave us His only begotten Son. Consequently, the Son decided to give us – or to obtain for us – the Holy Spirit.

> *If you love me, you will obey what I command. And I will ask the Father, and he will give you another Counselor to be with you forever the Spirit of truth. The world cannot accept him, because it neither sees him nor knows him. But you know him, for he lives with you and will be in you. (John 14:15-17)*

In other words, if God had not given us His Son, we would not have been able to receive the Holy Spirit. Because the Son obtained the Holy Spirit for us, we benefit mentally (as far as our souls are concerned), we benefit physically (as far as our bodies are concerned), and we benefit spiritually, too.

He tells us what the Holy Spirit will do for us:

> *But the Counselor, the Holy Spirit, whom the Father will send in my name, will teach you all things and will remind you of everything I have said to you. (John 14:26)*

The Holy Spirit will teach us all things and He will remind us of the things that we have learned.

> *I have much more to say to you, more than you can now bear. But when he, the Spirit of truth, comes, he will guide you into all truth. He will not speak on his own; he will speak only what he hears, and he will tell you what is yet to come. (John 16:12-13)*

THE SPIRIT OF TRUTH

The Holy Spirit will guide us into all truth. The Holy Spirit will guide us, step by step, into the hidden truths in the Bible. In the past, I would just read the Bible like any book, blind to the fact that from every verse, you can write a book of significant inspiration. I have been able to discover the hidden truths in the Bible through the help of the Holy Spirit.

Physically, the Holy Spirit keeps our bodies strong and healthy. If your body is always aching, and you do not overwork yourself, you may need to check whether your spiritual tank is still full of the Holy Spirit or not.

> *And if the Spirit of him who raised Jesus from the dead is living in you, he who raised Christ from the dead will also give life to your mortal bodies through his Spirit, who lives in you. (Romans 8:11)*

If the Holy Spirit is in you, He revs you up. He renews your body from within, on a constant basis. Ephesians tells us something else that the Holy Spirit says:

> *In order that we, who were the first to hope in Christ, might be for the praise of his glory. And you also were included in Christ when you heard the word of truth, the gospel of your salvation. Having believed, you were marked in him with a seal the promised Holy Spirit.*
> *(Ephesians 1:12-13)*

When you surrender your life to Jesus Christ and become baptized in the Holy Spirit, the seal of God is stamped on your forehead. You cannot see it, but it is there. When Satan's cohorts see you, they know you. This is why you should not run away from them. They are supposed to run when they see you.

Spiritually, because the Holy Spirit has been given to us, we can get power.

> *But you will receive power when the Holy Spirit comes on you; and you will be my witnesses in Jerusalem, and in all Judea and Samaria, and to the ends of the earth.*
> *(Acts 1:8)*

THE TREASURE WE HAVE

The Holy Spirit is our witnessing gear, even in difficult situations.

> *On my account you will be brought before governors and kings as witnesses to them and to the Gentiles. But when they arrest you, do not worry about what to say or how to say it. At that time you will be given what to say for it will not be you speaking, but the Spirit of your Father speaking through you. (Matthew 10:18-20)*

The Holy Spirit is your inspiration for public speaking. The boldness to witness comes from the Holy Spirit. With the power of the Holy Spirit, you can move mountains.

> *But we have this treasure in jars of clay to show that this all-surpassing power is from God and not from us.*
> *(2 Corinthians 4:7)*

Here is the secret of a victorious Christian life. The treasure we have in our bodies is the Holy Spirit. Once you have the Holy Spirit, you shall always be triumphant.

FROM GLORY TO GLORY

2 Corinthians tells us of one of the most beautiful things the Holy Spirit can do in our lives.

> *And we, who with unveiled faces all reflect the Lord's glory, are being transformed into his likeness with ever increasing glory, which comes from the Lord, who is the Spirit. (2 Corinthians 3:18)*

What changes us from glory to glory? It is the Spirit of the Lord. He does it by showing us the divine mirror of the Word of God. By looking at that mirror, we discover things that are still wrong in our lives and correct them. Gradually, you will find yourself becoming more and more like Jesus. Just like a mirror, the Word of God shows your split spiritual image. If you are wise, you will make the necessary changes, immediately.

Whenever the Word of God challenges your life, you need to reform, immediately. There are some people who have been Christians for several years but have never had any life-changing experience. The reason is simple: The moment the Word of God begins to hammer in the truth, challenging them to get real with God, instead of adjusting, they become angry. What they have refused to accept is that the Word of God is designed to change you, with the help of the Holy Spirit.

DON'T MOVE UNTIL...

If you have been born again and you have not been baptized in the Holy Spirit, you need to make a quick demand from God immediately. Jesus admonishes us not to venture an inch in our Christian race without the Holy Spirit.

> *I am going to send you what my Father has promised; but stay in the city until you have been clothed with power from on high. (Luke 24:49)*

Don't you dare move without the Holy Spirit. If you have already been baptized in the Holy Spirit, your cry should be like that of David:

> *Create in me a pure heart, O God, and renew a steadfast spirit within me. Do not cast me from your presence or take your Holy Spirit from me. (Psalm 51:10-11)*

When the Holy Spirit departed from Samson, he became an ordinary man. With the Holy Spirit, he could tear lions in pieces. He could destroy a thousand men with the jawbone of an ass. When his immoral lifestyle chased the Holy Spirit away, he became a deflated soccer ball and a bad joke. He became empty, useless and defeated.

LOVE GIVES POWER

God gave His Son. His Son gave us the Holy Spirit, and through the Holy Spirit, we get power. The word "power" – as it is used in Acts 1:8 – is dunamis, in the original Greek language. It is from this word that we have the word, dynamite. Dynamite is used to blast rocks. This is the kind of power that God says we will have when we receive the Holy Ghost.

What is this power for? The answer is in Luke:

> *I have given you authority to trample on snakes and scorpions and to overcome all the power of the enemy; nothing will harm you. (Luke 10:19)*

If this is the only promise that Jesus Christ gave us, it is enough to rejoice in. This is absolute security. He says nothing evil has power over us. Isaiah says that this power is for defense.

> *"No weapon forged against you will prevail, and you will refute every tongue that accuses you. This is the heritage*

> *of the servants of the LORD, and this is their vindication from me," declares the LORD. (Isaiah 54:17)*

Defense can be used in two formats. One is passive defense and the other is active defense. The latter was the type David used against Goliath.

The power is also used for offense. Meaning, don't even wait for the enemy to strike before you attack. This is what God expects you to do:

> *And these signs will accompany those who believe: In my name they will drive out demons; they will speak in new tongues; They will pick up snakes with their hands; and when they drink deadly poison, it will not hurt them at all; they will place their hands on sick people, and they will get well. (Mark 16:17-18)*

You are to cast out demons, whether they like it or not. We are to become terrors to the enemy. You are to cast out demons and not accommodate them. I think that when a Christian says he or she is demon possessed, the genuineness of his or her salvation is suspect. How can you say Jesus Christ dwells in you side by side with a demon? Light and darkness do not co-habit. If you are truly born-again, what my Bible tells me about you is written in Colossians:

> *To them God has chosen to make known among the Gentiles the glorious riches of this mystery, which is Christ in you, the hope of glory. (Colossians 1:27)*

You have overcome them because greater is He that is in you than he that is in the world or haven't you read:

> *You, dear children, are from God and have overcome them, because the one who is in you is greater than the one who is in the world. (1 John 4:4)*

DON'T TOLERATE IT!

To take up serpents means that you will challenge the devil.

You are the only one who can allow evil forces to come near you. They will torment you for as long as you permit them. In Acts 13:8-12, Paul was preaching to a governor when this sorcerer, Bar-Jesus, started distracting the attention of the governor and opposing Paul. This went on until Paul turned to him and decreed that he should be blind for a season. He became blind immediately. Whatever you tolerate will stay with you.

Many people have been indoctrinated to believe that they are desperate deliverance candidates. They lengthen deliverance queues every time. Wild pursuits of deliverance sessions open the door of your life for more demons to come in. The deliverance becomes continuous. You then become like someone who has a very old and cranky car which has to visit the repair shop all the time. Many people have become regular customers of deliverance ministers.

How do we operate the power given to us by the Holy Spirit?

> *My people are destroyed from lack of knowledge. "Because you have rejected knowledge, I also reject you as my priests; because you have ignored the law of your God, I also will ignore your children." (Hosea 4:6)*

> *So I said, "Wisdom is better than strength. But the poor man's wisdom is despised, and his words are no longer heeded." (Ecclesiastes 9:16)*

OPERATE THE POWER

We need to know how to operate the power that the Almighty God has made available to us. Many of us have the power of the Almighty God inside us, waiting to be released. The Bible tells us how to release the power.

> *Submit yourselves, then, to God. Resist the devil, and he will flee from you. (James 4:7)*

Most of us read only the second part of the verse that tells us to resist the devil. When we resist the devil, nothing happens because we have not bothered to fulfill the preceding condition that we must submit to God. We are talking of not just submitting an area of your life to God but submitting your entire life. Many of us still argue with God. The secret of access to God's power is submission to God.

Here is the story of a widow who met with the challenge of submission.

> *Then the word of the LORD came to him: "Go at once to Zarephath of Sidon and stay there. I have commanded a widow in that place to supply you with food." So he went to Zarephath. When he came to the town gate, a widow was there gathering sticks. He called to her and asked, "Would you bring me a little water in a jar so I may have a drink?" As she was going to get it, he called, "And bring me, please, a piece of bread." As surely as the LORD your God lives," she replied, '1 don't have any bread - only a handful of flour in a jar and a little oil in a jug. I am gathering a few sticks to take home and make a meal for myself and my son, that we may eat it and die." Elijah said to her, "Don't be afraid. Go home and do as you have said. But first make a small cake of bread for me from what you have and bring it to me, and then make something for yourself and your son. For this is what the LORD, the God of Israel, says: 'The jar of flour will not be used up and the jug of oil will not run dry until the day the LORD gives rain on the land." She went away and did as Elijah had told her. So there was food every day for Elijah and for the woman and her family. For the jar of flour was not used up and the jug of oil did not run dry, in keeping with the word of the LORD spoken by Elijah.*
> *(1 Kings 17:8-16)*

This is simply an epic story of submission. The man of God asked her to submit and she did. She surrendered all she had, at a time of great adversity. She put her life and the life of her son on the line.

She submitted and she never lacked anything for the rest of her life. She lost all worries and fears of the future.

Submit to the Almighty. Dedicate your children to the Almighty God. Do the same with your business. Give everything in your life over to the Almighty God and relax. If He wants to take anything, let Him take it. I want you to ask God to take over everything that you have. However, you must remember that He will answer your prayer. Therefore, if you are not really ready, do not bother to say this prayer. After surrendering, you can now resist the devil. If you are not yet born-again, giving your life to Jesus Christ is the first step to giving God your all.

CHAPTER 8
LOVE GIVES GENEROUSLY

The God Who can give His only begotten Son, must be a very generous Giver with a big "G". If you have only one thing and you are willing to give it away, you must be a very generous giver, as well. This Giver tells us that He is the Lord God Almighty.

> *When Abram was ninety-nine years old, the LORD appeared to him and said, 'I am God Almighty; walk before me and be blameless. (Genesis 17:1)*

In the original Greek language, it reads as Jehovah El-Shaddai. Jehovah El-Shaddai means the God who is more than enough.

When you study the nature of the God, you will find out that He is always doing more than you can ever ask for. For example, not only did He deliver the children of Israel out of Egypt, He drowned all their enemies. Not a single one was left.

> *Then the LORD said to Moses, "Stretch out your hand over the sea so that the waters may flow back over the Egyptians and their chariots and horsemen. "Moses stretched out his hand over the sea, and at daybreak the sea went back to its place. The Egyptians were fleeing toward it, and the LORD swept them into the sea. The water flowed back and covered the chariots and horsemen - the entire army of Pharaoh that had followed the Israelites into the sea. Not one of them survived. (Exodus 14:26-28)*

That's how He'll drown all your enemies too – that is, unless they repent and become godly brothers and sisters.

JEHOVAH EL-SHADDAI

In 2 Kings 4:1-7, there is a story of a widow who ran to a man of God for help. She was in debt and creditors had come to take her sons to the slave camp. All that the woman asked for was a financial breakthrough to clear her debts. However, when Jehovah El-Shaddai stepped in, not only did He pay off this woman's debt, she had enough money to live on for the rest of her life.

Many of us are still poor because we refuse to pray. I'm not talking about the five minute prayer, but the prayer that will shake the heavens. Jehovah El-Shaddai paid the debt of this widow and she never had financial problems again. How can we really serve God the way He should be served when we don't know how we are going to pay our bills?

I remember years ago, when we were building the auditorium at the Redemption Camp along the Lagos-Ibadan expressway. We needed some money for the carpenters, but the money was just not there. The carpenters wanted the money immediately, but I told them to wait. I handed the issue to God and fell asleep, because I had been praying all night. By the time I woke up, I met someone at my door, eating his breakfast. The first thought that came to my mind was that he must have a serious problem, to be blocking the entrance to my office. He told me that he had no problems. But, as he was eating his breakfast at home, God told him to go and give me some money. He handed over an envelope to me. After I had prayed God's blessings on him and he had gone, I opened the envelope and found well over what was needed for the carpenters. That was my God, Who is more than enough, in action. He gave me what I needed, with some to spare.

In 2 Kings 7:1-18, four lepers, who could not live within the society in good times, were still ostracized in war-induced famine. The adversity was so advanced that mothers ate their children. The lepers took bold steps to snoop around the enemy's camp, which they found empty of soldiers but full of booty. What they thought could be their last meal led to the beginning of their breakthrough. Before they told anyone else, they ate to their fill and buried enough gold and silver to last for the rest of their lives.

For those bogged down by bank loans, if only you would allow the fire of God to come into your bones, very soon, banks will owe you, because His name is Jehovah El-Shaddai. In 2 Chronicles 1:8-12, Solomon asked God for wisdom and understanding to be a good leader. God gave him wisdom and understanding and in addition, He gave Solomon wealth, fame, long life and victory over all his enemies. God kept on giving because He is Jehovah El-Shaddai.

In 2 Chronicles 20:24-25, three kings came against Jehoshaphat. Jehoshaphat cried to God for help. When God intervened, Jehoshaphat and his army spent three days carting away wealth into their treasury – without fighting their enemies. Jehoshaphat asked for deliverance, but God also gave him wealth.

That is not difficult to fathom because He is Jehovah El-Shaddai, the God Who gave His only begotten Son to redeem the whole world. The Son He gave is also like His Father. This is why I am always surprised to see "children of God" who are not generous. They should behave like their Father if they are truly children of God. They should be generous to a fault, just like their Father, Jehovah El-Shaddai.

A crowd once gathered to hear Jesus in John 6:6-13. When He perceived that they could be hungry, He asked His disciples to feed them. All they could find was a little boy's lunch. The boy graciously gave his lunch away. Jesus blessed the food, thanked Almighty God and fed the people. There were twelve baskets left over after five thousand men, excluding women and children, were done eating. The Son is like His Father. He is also Jehovah El-Shaddai.

When you look through the Scriptures, you will see several passages telling you that the Lord God Almighty wants to give you more than you can ask for from Him.

> *No, in all these things we are more than conquerors through him who loved us. (Romans 8:37)*

God wants us to be more than conquerors, and not ordinary victors.

> *Now to him who is able to do immeasurably more than all we ask or imagine, according to his power that is at work within us. (Ephesians 3:20)*

God can give you those things that you are even afraid to ask from Him – or think about. It takes some Christians a lot of courage to pray that God give them a car. The good news is that He would give you a helicopter. You too can ask God to let your cup run over and to fill you to overflowing with the Holy Spirit.

You can ask Him to baptize you with fire so that when demons see you, they will see the consuming fire of God.

> *You prepare a table before me in the presence of my enemies. You anoint my head with oil, my cup overflows.*
> *(Psalm 23:5)*

> *I baptize you with water for repentance. But after me will come one who is more powerful than I whose sandals*

> *I am not fit to carry. He will baptize you with the Holy Spirit and with fire. (Matthew 3:11)*

Anybody can kick a football. However, nobody can kick a ball of fire. If you kick a ball of fire, you will get burnt. If you stand on a ball of fire, you will burn your feet. Ask the Holy Spirit to baptize you with fire. For many years, I avoided big family get-togethers in my hometown in the village, until I got baptized in the Holy Spirit and with fire. Now, those who had threatened to make demonic breakfast out of me run away from me. They begin to tremble when they see me.

In Acts 19:11-12, the Bible tells us that God performed special miracles by the hand of Paul. From his body, handkerchiefs and aprons were taken to the sick; and the sick subsequently got loosed from their demonic oppression and were healed. His very sweat was fire. Paul was just a mortal man like any other. He got born again just like anybody else. The only extraordinary ability he got was the baptism of fire from the Holy Ghost. He was also a prayer warrior. This is what you should strive to become.

LOVE GIVES WITHOUT LIMITS

When God gave us His only begotten Son, He gave us the ultimate present.

> *He who did not spare his own Son, but gave him up for us all - how will he not also, along with him, graciously give us all things? (Romans 8:32)*

The first Sunday of every new year is usually dubbed Thanksgiving. That is always a good time to take an inventory to see whether God did anything in our lives in the previous year worth thanking Him for.

I always advise that when it is time to thank God, your thanks offering should show Him what you think of what He has done. If He has done much, give Him much. If He has not done much, give Him little.

If He has not done anything at all, give Him so little that it would get Him to do something. God loves those who are honest. He does not like pretenders. Do not pretend that He has done something for you when He has not done anything. Do not give an offering to please the Pastor. Be honest with your God.

As for me, the reason I have stopped giving testimonies is because if I say what He has done for me, people will say God is partial. Where do I start? Is it the miracles that I have seen? Is it the growth of the church? Is it the peace and harmony in my home? Is it protection over my children? Is it the helping hand that God keeps sending to those close to me all over the world? Is it my own good health?

HE IS WORTHY TO BE PRAISED

There might be some people for whom God did nothing. I want to share a story to help you evaluate God's worthiness.

The wife of a man from the company of the prophets cried out to Elisha, "Your servant my husband is dead, and you know that he revered the LORD. But now his creditor is coming to take my two boys as his slaves."

> *Elisha replied to her, "How can I help you? Tell me, what do you have in your house?" "Your servant has nothing there at all" she said, "except a little oil" Elisha said, "Go around and ask all your neighbors for empty jars. Don't ask for just a few. Then go inside and shut the door behind you and your sons. Pour oil into all the jars, and as each is filled, put it to one side." She left him and afterward shut the door behind her and her sons. They brought the jars to her and she kept pouring. When all the jars were full, she said to her son, "Bring me another one." But he replied, "There is not a jar left." Then the oil stopped flowing. She went and told the man of God, and he said, "Go, sell the oil and pay your debts. You and your sons can live on what is left." (2 Kings 4:1-7)*

This woman was so deep in debt that her children were almost incarcerated by her creditors. She ran to Elisha, the servant of the Most High, for help. Elisha asked her what she had in the house. The woman said she had nothing at all except one little pot of oil. If she had nothing, how did she manage to run to Elisha? What was it that she used to run to Elisha? She ran to Elisha on two good legs.

Ask the lame man at the Beautiful gate if legs are important (Acts 3:1-10). He wanted to join worshippers in the house of God. He wanted to dance and praise God, but he had no legs. Many of us have two good legs, yet we cannot dance for God. This woman said she had nothing. But how did she see to make her way to the house of Elisha? She had two good eyes. She should have asked Bartimaeus the importance of eyes (Mark 10:46-52). He was a blind man. When he came before the King of kings, and he was given the opportunity to ask for anything he wanted, he asked that his sight should be restored. He did not ask for anything else.

I pray you never go blind. Nothing can be as terrible as the loss of your sight. Satan has not succeeded in taking your eyes, yet you cannot praise God. Shame on you. This debtor woman said that she had nothing, yet she was able to tell the man of God her problem. How was she able to do this? It was because she had a mouth that she could use to talk.

> *O Lord, open my lips, and my mouth will declare your praise. (Psalm 51:15)*

We do not seem to know the value of some of the things God has given us. I pray that you will never be dumb, in the name of Jesus Christ. You can talk, yet you refuse to sing praises to God.

This debtor woman said she had nothing, yet in famine, she still had two strong boys. If those boys were sickly, no creditor would have wanted them. The children were so healthy that the creditors wanted them as a fair exchange for what they were owed. Yet, she said she had nothing. Despite what is happening in Nigeria – and all over the world – God still sustains you and your family. You should be grateful to God.

This debtor woman said she had nothing, yet she was able to get pots from neighbors, at short notice. This woman was living among wonderful neighbors. There are some of us who are living in hostile neighborhoods. There are some of us who are living among demonic lions of the spirit realm. It is the grace of God that preserves us. Should God's grace over our lives be taken away, for just one minute, I am sure that's enough time for satanic elements to eliminate us. There are enough dangers in your home and in your office to destroy you, ten times over, in one day. What about violent criminals? Have you given any thought to the dangers assassins pose? What about drunk drivers? You go out and come in safely, yet you cannot thank God?

She said she had nothing but a pot of oil. The Bible tells me that oil is for joy. I have joy and nobody can take it from me. I have the joy of salvation. The Bible tells me to rejoice in the Lord always.

This woman said she had nothing, but she had Elisha and the God of Elisha, as it were. The God of Elisha so loved us that He gave us His only begotten Son. I have Jesus. You have Jesus. We have the One Who is also known as Wonderful, Miracle, Counselor and Mighty God. We have the One Whose name is Everlasting Father – the same yesterday, today and tomorrow. We have the Prince of Peace. It does not matter what happens, it is going to be well with me. I know it is going to be well with you also.

As long as my hands can still move, I will clap for the Lord.

As long as I have my voice, I will sing and praise the Lord. As long as my legs are there, I will dance to His praise forever in Jesus' name. Amen.

Chapter 9
Love Gives Victory

For God so loved the world means for God so loved Adeboye and you too. This also means that you have a friend. Somebody loves you. God loves you sincerely, not for any hidden agenda. In fact, the Bible states that when we were yet sinners, Christ died for us. He loved you when you were His enemy. And, if you are now His child, you can be sure that He loves you even more. Because He loves us, we are more than conquerors.

> *No, in all these things we are more than conquerors through him who loved us. (Romans 8:37)*

Being more than a conqueror could mean several things. It could mean that you are greater than somebody who has conquered. In other words, before you begin the fight at all, you have won. Before you fight against the devil, you have already won the battle. Your victory is guaranteed by our elder brother, the Lord Jesus Chris,t Who has already defeated the devil. He has taken the teeth out of the Lion's mouth.

It could also mean that you have conquered more than once. In other words, it implies that you have more than one battle to fight. It means you keep on fighting and you keep on winning. So, being more than a conqueror could mean conquering more than once. As a matter of fact, the psalmist seems to support this definition.

> *A righteous man may have many troubles, but the LORD delivers him from them all. (Psalm 34:19)*

The enemy will chase you many times, but the Lord will deliver you all the time. It does not matter how many battles you have to fight, you have won even before you begin the fight.

PRAY CONTINUALLY

> *Is any one of you in trouble? He should pray. Is anyone happy? Let him sing songs of praise. (James 5:13)*

All you have to do to succeed and overcome, in every situation, is to pray. This is what the devil has being trying to make sure we do not do. As long as you are relying on someone else to do the praying for you, the devil knows he has got you. Pray on your own. He is your Father and you do not need any intermediary to get to Him. How often are you to pray?

> *Pray continually. (1 Thessalonians 5:17)*

Just keep on praying. Pray when all is well. Pray when all is not well. Pray when you are happy. Pray when you are afflicted. Pray when you are about to eat. Pray when you have finished eating. Keep on praying. The moment you begin to pray, you will just find that you go from victory to victory. If you do not know how to pray, then you should refer to Romans:

> *In the same way, the Spirit helps us in our weakness. We do not know what we ought to pray for, but the Spirit himself intercedes for us with groans that words cannot express. (Romans 8:26)*

If Paul, the apostle, could say that he does not know how to pray, then you should not feel too put down that you do not know how to pray. In some other passages of Scripture, Paul admitted that he could pray in tongues more than all the other apostles. We do not know how to pray, but thank God for the Holy Spirit. He comes in to help us. Many times, you do not even know what words would make a prayer. There is One who understands all situations and His name is the Holy Spirit.

PRAY CORRECTLY

How do we pray correctly? We all know that the Bible states that we should glorify God. How many people really thank God for fifty minutes out of a sixty-minute prayer session? If you do this, you must be very special. In a one-hour prayer session, most of us thank God for five minutes and then we bombard Him with requests the rest of the time.

The Bible gives us insight into how the Holy Spirit would rather have us pray.

> *But when he, the Spirit of truth, comes, he will guide you into all truth. He will not speak on his own; he will speak only what he hears, and he will tell you what is yet to come. He will bring glory to me by taking from what is mine and making it known to you. (John 16:13-14)*

Jesus Christ said that the Holy Spirit will glorify Him. When you pray in tongues, I can assure you that 99% of the time you are just praising God and glorifying Him. The Holy Spirit brings in your request during the remaining 10% and the request will be granted. When you are praying in tongues, the Holy Spirit goes between you and Jesus Christ.

In 1 John 5:14-15, we read that if we pray according to the will of God, He hears us and gives us what we ask for. What is the will of God concerning what you ask for? You may not know it but the Holy Spirit knows.

> *And he who searches our hearts knows the mind of the Spirit, because the Spirit intercedes for the saints in accordance with God's will. (Romans 8:27)*

BELIEVING IS RECEIVING

The Holy Spirit prays through you, according to the will of God, and you will get the result you expect.

> *I tell you the truth, if anyone says to this mountain, 'Go, throw yourself into the sea,' and does not doubt in his heart but believes that what he says will happen, it will be done for him. Therefore I tell you, whatever you ask for in prayer, believe that you have received it, and it will be yours. (Mark 11:23-24)*

What you receive when you pray are the things you believe that you have received and not just the catalogue of things for which you have prayed. When you are praying about something, if all of a sudden you have the assurance that you have already received it, you will get it. Do not stop praying until you have the assurance that you have received what you have prayed for. The word of God says it will be to us according to our faith.

> *But you, dear friends, build yourselves up in your most holy faith and pray in the Holy Spirit. (Jude 20)*

When you pray in the Holy Ghost, you build up your faith.

CHAPTER 10
LOVE GIVES PURPOSEFULLY

In the past, I spent a lot of time pondering over why God would give His very best to His enemies. I can understand anyone giving the best to a friend. But it's strange, to say the least, to give your best to your enemy. After a lot of prayers and seeking the face of the Lord, I discovered that the principal reason God did this was the law of harvest. The law of harvest says whatever you sow you will reap.

> *Do not be deceived: God cannot be mocked. A man reaps what he sows. (Galatians 6:7)*

> *By their fruit you will recognize them. Do people pick grapes from thorn bushes, or figs from thistles?*
> *(Matthew 7:16)*

Combine these two Scriptures and it becomes clear that the exact thing you sow is what you will reap. In other words, if you sow yam, you are not going to reap groundnut. The law of harvest also says that what you sow is less than what you harvest.

> *They sow the wind and reap the whirlwind. The stalk has no head; it will produce no flour. Were it to yield grain, foreigners would swallow it up. (Hosea 8:7)*

If you sow just one seed, you are not going to harvest one seed. Farmers can confirm that. When God the Father gave His only begotten Son, He was sowing so that that He could reap. He had one begotten Son and He wanted many more sons. The Bible tells us that God gave us Jesus Christ because He wanted to bring many sons to glory.

> *In bringing many sons to glory, it was fitting that God, for whom and through whom everything exists, should make the author of their salvation perfect through suffering. (Hebrews 2:10)*

> *But as many as received him, to them gave he power to become the sons of God, even to them that believe on his name. (John 1:12 KJV)*

I also wondered why Jesus Christ agreed to die. Jesus Christ made it clear that He laid down His life voluntarily.

> *The reason my Father loves me is that I lay down my life - only to take it up again. No one takes it from me, but I lay it down of my own accord. I have authority to lay it down and authority to take it up again. This command I received from my Father. (John 10:17-18)*

In other words, even when God the Father sent Him into the world, He was given the option not to die. Why did Jesus choose to die?

> *Greater love has no one than this, that he lay down his life for his friends. (John 15:13)*

He laid down His life for His friends because He wanted to multiply Himself. He sowed Himself so that there can be many more like Him.

> *I tell you the truth, anyone who has faith in me will do what I have been doing. He will do even greater things than these, because I am going to the Father. (John 14:12)*

Because He died and sowed Himself, as many as will believe in Him will be able to do the things that He did and even much more. Why did the Holy Spirit allow Jesus Christ to die? The Bible tells us clearly that it is with the help of the Holy Spirit that Jesus died.

The Holy Spirit and Jesus Christ are the best partners.

> *How God anointed Jesus of Nazareth with the Holy Spirit and power, and he went around doing good and healing all who were under the power of the devil, because God was with him. (Acts 10:38)*

They were partners in progress. They were partners in the Ministry. The Holy Spirit allowed His Partner to die because He knew that if He was able to sow one Partner, He would get more partners from the harvest that is sure to follow.

> *But I tell you the truth: It is for your good that I am going away. Unless I go away, the Counselor will not come to you; but if I go, I will send him to you. (John 16:7)*

SONS-FRIEND-PARTNERS

As long as Jesus Christ was around, the Holy Spirit was obligated to Him. The Holy Spirit could only work with this Partner as long as He was around. To harvest other partners, Jesus Christ had to be sowed. Today, the Holy Spirit has many partners. Because God so loved the world, He gave His only begotten Son, we have three things planned for our lives:

1. God the Father wants to make us glorious children.
2. God the Son wants to make us glorious friends.
3. The Holy Spirit wants to make us glorious partners.

We have certain things to do for these plans of God to be fulfilled. This is what God the Father requires from us:

> *For those God foreknew he also predestined to be conformed to the likeness of his Son, that he might be the firstborn among many brothers. (Romans 8:29)*

He wants us to be conformed to the image of His Son. He is ready to make us glorious children but Jesus Christ will be His First Son while we take our positions behind Him. People should look at you and Jesus Christ and see that both of you are from the same Father. You must be ready to conform to the image of Jesus Christ, otherwise, you will have to tell everybody why you are a black sheep.

What does God the Son require from us to be His friends?

> *You are my friends if you do what I command.*
> *(John 15:14)*

Jesus Christ is ready to accept you as His friend but only birds of the same feather flock together. You have no problems as long as you do whatever He tells you. What are the things Jesus Christ wants you to do? One is for us to love one another. A second one is bear fruit.

> *You did not choose me, but I chose you and appointed you to go and bear fruit – fruit that will last. Then the Father will give you whatever you ask in my name.*
> *(John 15:16)*

He wants you to love all the brethren, to win souls and to make sure that you follow them up until they become established – whatever the cost.

CONTROLLING YOUR TONGUE

What else does the Holy Spirit want from you? He wants your tongue. On the day of Pentecost, the apostles were all speaking in new tongues, as the Spirit gave them utterance.

> *When the day of Pentecost came, they were all together in one place. Suddenly a sound like the blowing of a violent wind came from heaven and filled the whole house where they were sitting. They saw what seemed to be tongues of fire that separated and came to rest on each of them. All of them were filled with the Holy Spirit and began to speak in other tongues as the Spirit enabled them. (Acts 2:1-4)*

In other words, they surrendered their tongues to the Holy Spirit and He used their tongues to do what He wanted to do. Why would the Holy Spirit want your tongue? Whoever controls your tongue, controls you.

> *We all stumble in many ways. If anyone is never at fault in what he says, he is a perfect man, able to keep his whole body in check. When we put bits into the mouths of horses to make them obey us, we can turn the whole animal. Or take ships as an example. Although they are so large and are driven by strong winds, they are steered by a very small rudder wherever the pilot wants to go. Likewise the tongue is a small part of the body, but it makes great boasts. Consider what a great forest is set on fire by a small spark. The tongue also is a fire, a world of evil among the parts of the body. It corrupts the whole person, sets the whole course of his life on fire, and is itself set on fire by hell. All kinds of animals, birds, reptiles and creatures of the sea are being tamed and have been tamed by man, but no man can tame the tongue. It is a restless evil, full of deadly poison.*
> *(James 3:2-8)*

Your tongue is the steering wheel of your body and your life. The moment the Holy Spirit gets control of your tongue, He will use it to witness. Jesus Christ also said when the Holy Spirit comes, He shall glorify Him – with your tongue of course. Moreover, once the Holy Spirit gets control of your tongue, He will be able to get you to pray without ceasing, according to 1 Thessalonians 5:17, which challenges us to "Pray continually."

The sure-fire route to pray without ceasing is by praying in the spirit. If you are praying in your understanding, by the time you have prayed for three hours, you would have long been finished asking God for what you want and repetitions would have set in. However, if you are praying in tongues, you can go on for seven or more hours because the Holy Spirit will keep on helping you out.

Do you want to be a glorious child of God? Do you want to be a glorious friend of Jesus Christ? Are you ready to be a glorious partner of the Holy Spirit? God purposely gave His son for you. The choice to purposely serve God is yours.

Chapter 11
Love Gives Absolutely

If Jesus Christ were the only Gift God gave us, it would be wonderful enough, because He is the only begotten Son of the Father. The man who gives you the only thing he has must be very kind and generous, to the hilt. In the case of the Father, He had only one begotten Son and He gave Him out. However, this is not all that He did.

> *As soon as Jesus was baptized, he went up out of the water. At that moment heaven was opened, and he saw the Spirit of God descending like a dove and lighting on him. And a voice from heaven said, "This is my Son, whom I love; with him I am well pleased."*
> *(Matthew 3:16-17)*

For our sakes, God the Father decided that not only would He send God the Son, He would also send God the Holy Spirit. He demonstrated His willingness to stay alone in Heaven to give our salvation all that it required.

> *God anointed Jesus of Nazareth with the Holy Spirit and power, and how he went around doing good and healing all who were under the power of the devil, because God was with him. (Acts 10:38)*

The Almighty God felt that even sending His Son into the world is not enough and that Jesus needed a partner – God the Holy Spirit – to seal our salvation. In Isaiah, we find the reason why the Holy Spirit had to join Jesus Christ.

> *The Spirit of the Sovereign LORD is on me, because the LORD has anointed me to preach good news to the poor. He has sent me to bind up the brokenhearted, to proclaim freedom for the captives and release from darkness for the prisoners, to proclaim the year of the LORD's favor and the day of vengeance of our God, to comfort all who mourn, and provide for those who grieve in Zion – to bestow on them a crown of beauty instead of ashes, the oil of gladness instead of mourning, and a garment of praise instead of a spirit of despair. They will be called oaks of righteousness, a planting of the LORD for the display of his splendor. (Isaiah 61:1-3)*

BEAUTY FOR ASHES

We will concentrate on the last verse. Until you are born-again, you are not beautiful. Physical beauty is vanity. Before you became a believer, your self-esteem must have been far from satisfactory. Suddenly, you received salvation and the glory of God came upon you and you did not care what others thought of you. You suddenly discovered that you were beautiful.

> *For the LORD takes delight in his people; he crowns the humble with salvation. (Psalm 149:4)*

Salvation comes with beauty – guaranteed. What you called beauty before you were born-again were in fact, ashes. Let someone outside the Kingdom of God know that when they become born again, God gives them beauty that lasts forever.

Here is a little bit of God's definition of beauty.

> *Wives, in the same way be submissive to your husbands so that, if any of them do not believe the word, they may be won over without words by the behavior of their wives, when they see the purity and reverence of your lives. Your beauty should not come from outward adornment, such as braided hair and the wearing of gold jewelry and fine clothes. Instead, it should be that of your inner self, the unfading beauty of a gentle and quiet spirit, which is of great worth in God's sight. (1 Peter 3:1-4)*

Beauty to God points to things of the heart. Beauty, as far as God is concerned, is a combination of humility, meekness, obedience, love and generosity.

> *And the dust returns to the ground it came from, and the spirit returns to God who gave it. "Meaningless! Meaningless!" says the Teacher. "Everything is meaningless!*
> *(Ecclesiastes 12:7-8)*

> *Those who are wise will shine like the brightness of the heavens, and those who lead many to righteousness, like the stars for ever and ever. (Daniel 12:3)*

> *Then the righteous will shine like the sun in the kingdom of their Father. He who has ears, let him hear.*
> *(Matthew 13:43)*

Jesus Christ came to give us beauty for ashes. In the sight of God, everything that the world glorifies is like ashes. Until you receive Jesus Christ, you are bad news even if you do not realize it. You may not agree with this and say you are cool without Christ. You need Jesus to cleanse you from sins with His blood.

> *But if we walk in the light, as he is in the light, we have fellowship with one another, and the blood of Jesus, his Son, purifies us from all sin. (1 John 1:7)*

All of a sudden, you will find that you hunger and thirst for righteousness. Matthew declares:

> *Blessed are those who hunger and thirst for righteousness, for they will be filled. (Matthew 5:6)*

The anointing of God will also freely operate in your life.

> *You have loved righteousness and hated wickedness; therefore God, your God, has set you above your companions by anointing you with the oil of joy.*
> *(Hebrews 1:9)*

As soon as you begin to love the things that God loves, and you begin to hate the things that God hates, He will pour His oil of gladness on you, which is the anointing of the Holy Spirit. And, before you know it, you will begin to lay hands on the sick and they will recover. At first, the yokes in your own life will be broken.

> *In that day their burden will be lifted from your shoulders, their yoke from your neck; the yoke will be broken because you have grown so fat. (Isaiah 10:27)*

God has broken several yokes in my life. Before I was born again, apart from mathematics, I used to read several novels. The devil made sure that I read a particular novel entitled, They Used Magic. The book tells the story of the Second World War and how Hitler used magic in his operations.

This book put me in bondage for several years. From the book, I gathered some satanic information about certain days of the month considered unlucky days. I lost opportunities because I would not travel on the so-called unlucky days. When I became born-again, I discovered that the devil cannot even boast of designing a single day, not to mention making one.

Before I became a believer, I avoided visits to my ancestral or family home for thirteen years, for fear of some people who had threatened to hurt me. When I got born-again and the anointing broke this yoke, the tables turned. Those same spiritual bullies were the ones who ran away from me. Darkness must run from the light. Not only will the anointing break your yoke, it will also guarantee security and safety.

> *He allowed no one to oppress them; for their sake he rebuked kings: "Do not touch my anointed ones; do my prophets no harm. (Psalm 105:14-15)*

Little wonder then what David said:

> *You prepare a table before me in the presence of my enemies. You anoint my head with oil; my cup overflows.*
> *(Psalm 23:5)*

Belonging to God guarantees that your mourning turns into joy. Joy is different from happiness. Happiness happens. If you win a contract or you are promoted, you are happy because something positive has taken place. Because happiness depends on something happening, if something does not happen, there will be no happiness – we tend to be unhappy. There is no word like, "unjoy"' because joy does not depend on anything external but something internal. Joy is forever. Whether anything happens or not, you can still have joy. The Bible states that the joy of the Lord is our strength.

He also exchanged our spirit of heaviness for garments of praise. Before we were born-again, many of us usually woke up deep in depression or on the wrong sides of our beds, according to popular parlance. When we became born-again, the situation changed. We now know, without any doubt, that our future is secure. We now have a new name from our Lord Jesus Christ, and a new Father.

> *He came to that which was his own, but his own did not receive him. Yet to all who received him, to those*

> who believed in his name, he gave the right to become children of God. (John 1:11-12)

The Bible states that we had a despicable identity before we were born-again.

> You belong to your father, the devil, and you want to carry out your father's desire. He was a murderer from the beginning, not holding to the truth, for there is no truth in him. When he lies, he speaks his native language, for he is a liar and the father of lies. (John 8:44)

The moment we became born-again, we became sons of God.

> How great is the love the Father has lavished on us, that we should be called children of God! And that is what we are! The reason the world does not know us is that it did not know him. (1 John 3:1)

This new Father now guarantees us a new home. Before we were born-again, we were heading straight for Hell.

> Do not let your hearts be troubled. Trust in God trust also in me. In my Father's house are many rooms; if it were not so, I would have told you. I am going there to prepare a place for you. And if I go and prepare a place for you, I will come back and take you to be with me that you also may be where I am. (John 14:1-3)

SING A NEW SONG

We have mansions waiting for us in Heaven. How can you have a new name, a new Father and a new home without having a new song?

> I waited patiently for the LORD; he turned to me and heard my cry. He lifted me out of the slimy pit, out of the mud and mire; he set my feet on a rock and gave me a firm place to stand. He put a new song in my mouth, a hymn of praise to our God. Many will see and fear and put their trust in the LORD. (Psalm 40:1-3)

When you have a new name, you will begin to sing and rejoice that your name has been written in the Lamb's book of life. And you will rejoice in your new birth. When you realize that you have a new Father, you begin to sing that you have a Father who is the Almighty, King of kings and Lord of lords. The day it becomes dear to you that you have a home in Heaven, you are likely to start singing about your heavenly home and its beauty.

Why did God promote us from ashes to beauty, make us lose the "blues" for praise? Why did He remove the "heavy weights" off our spirit and give us freedom to achieve high-flying praise? It is that we might be trees of righteousness. The Lord saved our souls so that we will become trees of righteousness. To be a tree of righteousness means doing the right thing in every sphere of our lives according to the will of God.

> *Produce fruit in keeping with repentance. (Matthew 3:8)*

PRODUCE FRUITS OF RIGHTEOUSNESS

It is not enough for you to say that you are born-again. The fruit of change must show. People must see the fruit of repentance and righteousness in your life. Your righteousness must be such that people will be able to testify concerning you that there is a difference. Your righteousness must be legendary and keep tongues wagging.

> *By faith Enoch was taken from this life, so that he did not experience death; he could not be found, because God had taken him away. For before he was taken, he was commended as one who pleased God. (Hebrews 11:5)*

> *He replied, "Every plant that my heavenly Father has not planted will be pulled up by the roots." (Matthew 15:13)*

As soon as you begin to bear the fruit of righteousness, nobody will be able to uproot you. Nothing will shake you because you are planted by the Lord. Finally, we have these things so that He might be glorified. When the anointing of God on you breaks your yoke and the yokes of others whom you pray for, these people are not going to glorify you but God. When you now think of all what God has done for you, you will thankfully count your blessings like David did.

> *Praise the LORD, O my soul; all my inmost being, praise his holy name. Praise the LORD, O my soul, and forget not all his benefits – who forgives all your sins and heals all your diseases, who redeems your life from the pit and crowns you with love and compassion, who satisfies your desires with good things so that your youth is renewed like the eagle's. (Psalm 103:1-5)*

And you know what, you are bound to praise Him. Anyone who has received Jesus Christ will always be a bundle of praise. If you are not saved, you do not know what you are missing. Forgive me for telling you the truth. Anyone who is not born-again is ugly and going to ashes. If you come to Jesus, He will change your ashes to beauty. Anyone who is not born-again is suffering. Come, taste and see how good God is.

LOVE GIVES ALL

The Bible tells us that the Almighty God, Who has given us His only begotten Son, should be willing to give us anything for which we ask.

> *He who did not spare his own Son, but gave him up for us all - how will he not also, along with him, graciously give us all things? (Romans 8:32)*

When we look at our lives, we find that this is not always the case. We pray and at times, we do not get an answer or it does not come when and how we expect it. We then wonder why this happens, especially when you consider John 14:14, where Jesus Christ said if you ask anything in His name, He will do it. In Jeremiah 33:2-3, God said if you call upon Him in the time of trouble, He will answer. There are many possible reasons that our prayers are not answered.

SIN

If there is sin in your life, there is no need praying.

> Surely the arm of the LORD is not too short to save, nor his ear too dull to hear. But your iniquities have separated you from your God; your sins have hidden his face from you, so that he will not hear. (Isaiah 59:1-2)

If God does not hear, how can He answer? If you are living in sin and you are praying for God to bless you, He is not likely to answer your prayer. Your sin can hinder your prayer. This is why we preach holiness all the time. We are interested in results-oriented lifestyles.

INCOMPLETE OBEDIENCE

Many of us live in a semblance of obedience to God. But God prefers that you disobey Him completely rather than a halfhearted compliance. If you want to obey God at all, you must obey Him all the way. King Saul lost his kingdom because of partial obedience. God directed him to destroy the Amalekites – to wipe out everything: animal, man, woman and children. But, he spared the King, some livestock and some beautiful to behold materials. His mistakes permanently marked him for rejection by God and he lost his kingdom.

The reason why God wants total obedience is because He has said in His Word that He wants you to be hot or cold. If you are lukewarm, He will spit you out of His mouth. Nothing is as dangerous as a friend who is half-friend and half-enemy. If I know somebody to be my enemy, I will know how to deal with him. If you declare yourself to be my enemy, I will not come to your house to eat lest you poison me. If you are my friend, then I can come to your house and relax and eat anything. However, if you pretend to be my friend when you are not totally committed to me, there may be problems if we become too close. There are many of us living in half obedience according to the standards of the Word of God.

> *You did not choose me, but I chose you and appointed you to go and bear fruit – fruit that will last. Then the Father will give you whatever you ask in my name.*
> *(John 15:16)*

There are many who always witness Christ without follow-ups. We do not worry whether the fruit abide or not. Once you win a soul, your assignment over that soul does not end until either you or the soul returns to God. If you are a father or a mother and you give birth to a child, do you leave that child after five days and say you have done enough? You have to monitor them or else your obedience is incomplete.

ETERNAL LAWS

Your prayer may be hindered or denied because God has set in place certain conditions that are unchangeable and unless you meet those conditions perfectly, the desired results may never come. It is like going against the car manufacturer's manual that you should put water in your radiator and gasoline in your tank. If you put water and gas in your tank, your car will cough-up problems.

Many of us have been praying that God would prosper us – and God really wants to prosper us. Actually, praying for prosperity is a mere formality. It is the will of God, above all things, that we prosper and be in health – subject, of course, to the prosperity of our souls. God wants to prosper us but there is a prerequisite to prosperity. This is the law of harvest.

In Mark 10:28-30, Peter asked Jesus Christ what would be their reward for following Him. Jesus told him that if you give Him one thing in this world, while you are still alive, you will get a hundred and in the life to come, life everlasting. The Word of God is forever settled. If you give God one naira/dollar/pound sterling, you are not going to die until you get a hundred in return. If you give God zero, He will multiply it by hundred and you will get zero.

He said if you bring all the tithes into His house, he will open all the windows of Heaven and pour blessings which will overflow our storehouses or bank accounts.

> *Will a man rob God? Yet you rob me. "But you ask, 'How do we rob you?' "In tithes and offerings. You are under a curse – the whole nation of you – because you are robbing me. Bring the whole tithe into the storehouse, that there may be food in my house. Test me in this," says the LORD Almighty, "and see if I will not throw open the floodgates of heaven and pour out so much blessing that you will not have room enough for it."*
> (Malachi 3:8-10)

Some of us pay part of our tithes but not all. Some of us pay tithes on our salaries but we do not pay tithes on our second income. Furthermore, He did not ask us to send it but God expects us to bring it to Him. It is an insult to send your tithe to God. You have to bring your tithe, very humbly, because He may even refuse it. If He refuses your gift, you are finished.

GOD KNOWS THE FUTURE

God is the Alpha and Omega – the beginning and the end. It is possible that if He answers a particular prayer the way you want it, there would be severe consequences, not necessarily for you but perhaps for other people. For example, if you pray for a brand new Mercedes Benz and God knows that you are a fast driver, He may not give you this particular car so that you will not kill anyone. He may give you a previously owned car that you will not drive fast.

In 2 Kings 20, God sent a message to Hezekiah, who was on his sick bed, to put his house in order because it was time for him to pass on from the earth. Hezekiah said he did not want to die yet. God agreed and gave him fifteen more years to live.

Some kings, who were his enemies, came pretending that they were his friends. He took them on a royal tour around his palace and national treasuries. God sent a message to him again that the visitors would one-day carry away everything Hezekiah displayed in his palace. When Hezekiah heard this, he wished he had died. Three years later, he had a baby boy and rejoiced. Twelve years later, his extra fifteen years were over and he died.

This boy became king (2 Kings 21) and he did so much evil that he painted Jerusalem red with the blood of the innocent. The Almighty God said He would forsake His inheritance – Israel. If his father had died when he was meant to die, such an evil-doer would never have been born.

If God had answered the prayer of Jesus Christ at the Garden of Gethsemane, where would you be today? Thank God that the blood of Jesus Christ cleanses us from all sins.

SOMETHING SUPERIOR

God may not answer your prayer because He has something far more superior in store for you than what you were asking for. You may be asking Him for a bicycle while He wants to give you a car. You may be asking for a husband and He may want to be your Husband. There is another reason why God refused to answer Jesus' prayer in the Garden of Gethsemane. It was because God had decided to give Jesus Christ a Name that is above every other name.

> *And being found in appearance as a man, he humbled himself and became obedient to death – even death on a cross! Therefore God exalted him to the highest place and gave him the name that is above every name, that at the name of Jesus every knee should bow, in heaven and on earth and under the earth. (Philippians 2:8-10)*

He allowed Jesus to suffer in our place so He could have the beautiful things He had lined up for Him.

So what do we do after we have prayed and nothing seems to happen?

> *My heart is not proud, O LORD, my eyes are not haughty; I do not concern myself with great matters or things too wonderful for me. But I have stilled and quieted my soul; like a weaned child with its mother, like a weaned child is my soul within me. O Israel, put your hope in the LORD both now and forevermore. (Psalm 131)*

David used a very graphic illustration here of someone who has learned to trust in the Lord completely. He said that he is like a child who is weaned by the mother and suddenly the breast milk is taken away. When your mother took away the milk from you it was because your mother had a better plan for you. What kind of child is breast fed at ten? Only an odd and abnormal one.

There is no doubt about it that God loves you. He loves you so much that He gave you His only begotten Son. If you have any doubt about the fact that God loves you, this often quoted Scripture should put your mind at rest.

> *For God so loved the world that he gave his one and only Son, that whoever believes in him shall not perish but have eternal life. (John 3:16)*

Therefore, if He who loves you more than your mother did – decides to deny you of anything, then it must be for your own good. (That is, of course, with the exception of the previous five reasons.) So just rest in Him.

This is not to say that you should not pray. This is not an excuse for laziness. Before you can stop praying for any particular thing, pray at least three times, as Jesus did. He prayed until His sweat was like blood. If you pray powerfully and nothing happens then you can rest your case and wait on Him.

If you are not yet born-again, the first hindrance to your prayer is sin. Until you are washed in the blood of the Lamb, your sin will hinder your prayers. You can settle the issue of your salvation today.

CHAPTER 12
LOVE MAKES A WAY

I have discovered that the basis for prayer is John 3:16. It is true that the basis for prayer is the Word of God but Who is the Word of God?

> *In the beginning was the Word and the Word was with God and the Word was God... The Word became flesh and made his dwelling among us. We have seen his glory, the glory of the One and Only, who came from the Father, full of grace and truth. (John 1:1, 14)*

So, Jesus Christ is the Word of God. Why do I say that the basis for prayer is John 3:16? First, no prayer is acceptable or complete without praise. In Luke 2:13-14, we are told that at the birth of Jesus Christ, even the angels praised God, when He gave us His Son.

When you praise someone, you tell him who he is, what he can do or you tell him how pleasant he is. The greatest reason for praising the Almighty God, that I know, is that He gave us His only begotten

Son. Without Jesus Christ, we could not have been saved. Before you go to God for anything at all, the two things that are essential to take along are praises and thanksgiving. Why do we need to give God thanks?

> *Give thanks to the LORD, call on his name; make known among the nations what he has done. (Psalm 105:1)*

When you thank God, you thank Him for all that He has done. You can summarize everything that God did for you by saying He gave you His Son. The basis for our thanksgiving is John 3:16.

When you enter into the presence of God with thanksgiving – if you are a seasoned prayer warrior – what you want to do is to intercede for those who are precious to you. God does not want anyone to perish.

> *The Lord is not slow in keeping his promise, as some understand slowness. He is patient with you, not wanting anyone to perish, but everyone to come to repentance.*
> *(2 Peter 3:9)*

Fundamental to this fact is John 3:16.

Another type of prayer is supplication. Many of us are good in this area – big time beggars, when it comes to prayer. Prayer of supplication is based on the following Scripture:

> *He who did not spare his own Son, but gave him up for us all – how will he not also, along with him, graciously give us all things? (Romans 8:32)*

We supplicate because we know that the One Who gave His only begotten Son will give anything else.

There are three kinds of prayers in progression: asking, seeking and knocking. God the Son taught us about asking, seeking and knocking.

ASKING

> *So I say to you: Ask and it will be given to you; seek and you will find; knock and the door will be opened to you. For everyone who asks receives; he who seeks finds; and to him who knocks, the door will be opened.*
> *(Luke 11:9-10)*

Asking is based on the fact that we have John 3:16 because in John 14:14, Jesus Christ said if you ask anything in His name, you will receive. If God had not given us Jesus Christ, you would not be able to ask in His name.

SEEKING

On seeking, the psalmist tells us this:

> *The lions may grow weak and hungry, but those who seek the LORD lack no good thing. (Psalm 34:10)*

If God had not given us Jesus Christ, how could you seek Him? If "Lord", in this context, is referring to God Almighty, when you seek Him, you know you already have the best, according to John 3:16. The One who made the "Best" available will surely make the "good" available.

How can you knock on a door when you do not know where the door is?

> *I am the door. If anyone enters by Me, he will be saved, and will go in and out and find pasture. (John 10:9 NKJV)*

If you need something from someone who has what you want – and can give it to you – you must have one essential thing. This is the boldness to go to the fellow to ask. According to Hebrews, we have boldness to enter into the presence of God, by the blood of Jesus Christ, even though He is a consuming fire.

> *Therefore, brothers, since we have confidence to enter the Most Holy Place by the blood of Jesus.*
> *(Hebrews 10:19)*

Many times, when you get on your knees to pray, two things step in: doubt and accusations from the enemy. The enemy has you questioning your justification to ask or receive anything from God. For example, if you are trusting God for a child, the devil may remind you that when you were younger, you aborted three pregnancies. The devil may tell you that God has already given you all the children in His "quota" for you. There is no prayer poison more poignant than this. However, God gave His only begotten Son and we can stand on this Scripture:

> *But if we walk in the light, as he is in the light, we have fellowship with one another, and the blood of Jesus, his Son, purifies us from all sin. (1 John 1:7)*

When you kneel down to pray and the devil taunts you, all you need to do is to remind him that the blood of Jesus has cleansed you from all sin.

Chapter 13
The Greatest Joy

Once in a while, a man receives a gift that changes his life. Many of us have received such gifts. These gifts include money, children, a wife, and so on. The greatest gift ever given, was Jesus Christ. This Gift changed the world, Heaven and Hell. When Jesus Christ was born, an angel said that from that time on, there will be peace and goodwill towards all men.

> *Now there were in the same country shepherds living out in the fields, keeping watch over their flock by night. And behold, an angel of the Lord stood before them, and the glory of the Lord shone around them, and they were greatly afraid. Then the angel said to them, "Do not be afraid, for behold, I bring you good tidings of great joy which will be to all people. For there is born to you this day in the city of David a Savior, who is Christ the Lord. And this will be the sign to you: You will find a Babe*

> *wrapped in swaddling cloths, lying in a manger." And suddenly there was with the angel a multitude of the heavenly host praising God and saying: "Glory to God in the highest, And on earth peace, goodwill toward men!"*
> *(Luke 2:8-14 NKJV)*

From the day Jesus Christ was given to the world, even the world's calendar changed. People now talk of years before Christ and years after Christ – BC or AD. When Jesus Christ was given to us as a gift, things changed in Hell.

> *I am the Living One; I was dead, and behold I am alive for ever and ever! And I hold the keys of death and Hades.*
> *(Revelation 1:18)*

Before He was given to us, the superintendent of Hell was Satan. When Jesus came, He took the keys of death and Hell.

THE CHAIN REACTION

When He was given to us, Heaven was changed, according to John 1:1, 14. Before He was given to us, He was the Word, living with God in Heaven. But, when He came into the world, He became flesh. He went back to Heaven as a man. This changed Heaven.

> *For there is one God and one mediator between God and men, the man Christ Jesus. (1 Timothy 2:5)*

Jesus Christ became a one-of-a-kind Mediator because never has a man mediated between God and His creation. When you receive this Gift, whether you like it or not, your life will change. That is as certain as it is written:

> *Therefore, if anyone is in Christ, he is a new creation; the old has gone, the new has come! (2 Corinthians 5:17)*

When you receive a gift that changes your life, there is bound to be a reaction. For example, when Jesus Christ got the keys of death and Hell from Satan, Hell reacted. Let's get a replay of what happened:

> *Finally, be strong in the Lord and in his mighty power. Put on the full armor of God so that you can take your stand against the devil's schemes. For our struggle is not against flesh and blood, but against the rulers, against the authorities, against the powers of this dark world and against the spiritual forces of evil in the heavenly realms. (Ephesians 6:10-12)*

As soon as Satan discovered that he could not get Jesus and had lost his powers, he gathered all his angels together to fight the followers of Jesus Christ.

The earth also reacted. Multitudes, all over the world, gather together regularly, praising the One who brought a change to their lives. That's the report contained in the Word of God:

> *After this I looked and there before me was a great multitude that no one could count, from every nation, tribe, people and language, standing before the throne and in front of the Lamb. They were wearing white robes and were holding palm branches in their hands. And they cried out in a loud voice: "Salvation belongs to our God, who sits on the throne, and to the Lamb."*
> *(Revelation 7:9-10)*

Heaven rejoiced:

> *All the angels were standing around the throne and around the elders and the four living creatures. They fell down on their faces before the throne and worshipped God, Saying: "Amen! Praise and glory and wisdom and thanks and honor and power and strength be to our God for ever and ever. Amen!" (Revelation 7:11-12)*

Heaven and earth join in praising Him while Hell is resisting Him. When you find it difficult to praise God, then you know to which camp you belong. You either belong to the multitude praising Him in Heaven and earth or you belong to those resisting Him.

"WHAT WOULD YOU HAVE ME DO?"

Anyone who has truly received this Gift from God, sooner or later, will respond by asking God what He wants done. Acts 9:1-5, when Jesus met Saul of Tarsus, on the way to Damascus, He asked why Paul was persecuting Him. Saul had to clarify His identity. As soon as He revealed Himself, Saul asked what He wanted him to do.

As a response to this eternally valuable gift He has given you, ask Him what He wants you to do. He told Peter that He would make him a fisher of men. He told Mary Magdalene that she would become His treasure. He said to the mad man of Gadarenes that he would be His evangelist. If you have received Jesus Christ it is time to ask Him to make plain your pre-ordained place in His kingdom. If you have not received Him, this Gift can change your life, so receive Him now.

Chapter 14
Accept the Love of God

There are two typical responses that greet a gift, particularly a gift for which you did not ask. You either receive it or you reject it. God gave us His only begotten Son, His best. Yet, some people have rejected Him.

> *He came to that which was his own, but his own did not receive him. (John 1:11)*

The very first people to reject Jesus Christ were HIS OWN PEOPLE. To refuse to accept Jesus Christ is to cheat yourself out of a lot of precious promises.

THE WAY

To reject Jesus Christ means to lose the Way – Jesus Christ is the Way out of any predicament.

> *Jesus answered, "1 am the way and the truth and the life. No one comes to the Father except through me."*
> *(John 14:6)*

Anyone who rejects the Way will go astray.

> *A man who strays from the path of understanding comes to rest in the company of the dead. (Proverbs 21:16)*

If God shows you the way and you turn your back on it, you will surely not arrive at any meaningful destination.

THE TRUTH

When you refuse to receive Jesus Christ, the Gift of God, then you have rejected the Truth. If you reject the Truth, automatically, you will buy into a lie.

> *For this reason God sends them a powerful delusion so that they will believe the lie and so that all will be condemned who have not believed the truth but have delighted in wickedness. (2 Thessalonians 2:11-12)*

THE LIFE

Anyone who rejects Jesus Christ rejects Life. To reject Life means to die – eternally and in every sense that matters.

> *Whoever believes in the Son has eternal life, but whoever rejects the Son will not see life, for God's wrath remains on him. (John 3:36)*

There are all kinds of death: physical death, financial death, marital death, mental death, spiritual death, and so on. When you have Jesus Christ, you have abundant life. Physically, you are alive. Mentally, spiritually and financially, you are alive if you have Jesus Christ.

THE LIGHT

Jesus Christ is the Light of the world. This means that if you reject Jesus Christ, you reject the Light. To refuse Light means to accept darkness.

> *When Jesus spoke again to the people, he said, "I am the light of the world. Whoever follows me will never walk in darkness, but will have the light of life." (John 8:12)*

If you refuse Jesus Christ, you will abide in darkness.

THE SHEPHERD

Jesus tells us that He is the Good Shepherd.

> *I am the good shepherd. The good shepherd lays down his life for the sheep. (John 10:11)*

If you refuse the Shepherd, you will become meat for the lion. The devil is the lawless lion according to the Word of God.

> *Be self-controlled and alert. Your enemy the devil prowls around like a roaring lion looking for someone to devour. (1 Peter 5:8)*

The Shepherd is there to guide and guard you. If you separate yourself from the Shepherd, the lion will prey on you.

THE SAVIOUR

Jesus Christ is the Saviour.

> *She will give birth to a son, and you are to give him the name Jesus, because he will save his people from their sins. (Matthew 1:21)*

If you reject the Saviour, your sins will remain. It is not enough to be called a believer; even demons believe. You cannot talk about Jesus Christ without talking about the cross. You cannot say that you are a Christian if you have not repented of your sins. Your being born-again must be accompanied by genuine repentance.

There are so many believers in church who are not converted. This is why we have so many demon-possessed people filling up churches every service. If you have really repented of your sins, you will sin no more. You will not want to offend the One who loves you. It is after you have really repented that salvation comes.

When salvation comes, the Saviour comes in, too. When the Saviour comes in, demons depart. When light comes in, darkness must disappear. There is no way for demons to stay in your life when Jesus Christ lives in you.

> *Some Pharisees who were with him heard him say this and asked, "What? Are we blind too? "Jesus said, "If you were blind, you would not be guilty of sin; but now that you claim you can see, your guilt remains. "*
> *(John 9:40-41)*

If you reject the Saviour, your sins will remain. If your sins remain, you will pray and there will be no answer.

THE CAPTAIN OF THE HOSTS

He is the Captain of the hosts of Heaven. If you reject Him, you reject the only One who can guarantee your victory.

> *Lift up your heads, O you gates; be lifted up, you ancient doors, that the King of glory may come in. Who is this King of glory? The LORD strong and mighty, the LORD mighty in battle. Lift up your heads, O you gates; lift them up, you ancient doors, that the King of glory may come in. Who is he, this King of glory? The LORD Almighty - he is the King of glory. (Psalm 24:7-10)*

Many are fighting in battles, seen and unseen, without knowing that they are in the midst of battle – a battle over their lives and life hereafter. Thank God for the Lord of hosts. He knows all the enemies and challenges you may not even know about.

> *What, then, shall we say in response to this? If God is for us, who can be against us? (Romans 8:31)*

If you refuse the Lord of hosts, you will live in perpetual defeat. It's as simple as that.

APPRECIATE THE GIFT

Receiving a gift generates two types of attitudes in us. You either appreciate the gift or you despise it. Some people receive Jesus Christ and hold Him in high esteem, as Paul did.

> *But whatever was to my profit I now consider loss for the sake of Christ. What is more, I consider everything a loss compared to the surpassing greatness of knowing Christ Jesus my Lord, for whose sake I have lost all things. I consider them rubbish, that I may gain Christ and be found in him, not having a righteousness of my own that comes from the law, but that which is through faith in Christ - the righteousness that comes from God and is by faith. I want to know Christ and the power of his resurrection and the fellowship of sharing in his sufferings, becoming like him in his death.*
> *(Philippians 3:7-10)*

No wonder, he was able to finish his course. It is not surprising that he was so powerful that his handkerchief was able to dismiss demons.

Many of us have received Jesus Christ but we do not hold Him in high esteem over everything that concerns us. We do not know how precious the gift of God is. Problems part ways with us to the degree to which we know and esteem Jesus Christ the gift of God. In Jesus Christ's earthly hometown, they did not appreciate Him. This is true according to His own testimony on the matter:

> *Coming to his hometown, he began teaching the people in their synagogue, and they were amazed "Where did this man get this wisdom and these miraculous powers?" they asked, "Isn't this the carpenter's son? Isn't his mother's name Mary, and aren't his brothers James, Joseph, Simon and Judas? Aren't all his sisters with us? Where then did this man get all these things?" And they took offense at him. But Jesus said to them, "Only in his hometown and in his own house is a prophet without honor." And he did not do many miracles there because of their lack of faith. (Matthew 13:54-58)*

Others ignore Him even though they have Him in their lives.

> *That day when evening came, he said to his disciples, "Let us go over to the other side. Leaving the crowd behind, they took him along, just as he was, in the boat. There were also other boats with him. A furious squall came up, and the waves broke over the boat, so that it was nearly swamped. Jesus was in the stern, sleeping on a cushion. The disciples woke him and said to him, "Teacher, don't you care if we drown?" He got up, rebuked the wind and said to the waves, "Quiet! Be still!" Then the wind died down and it was completely calm. He said to his disciples, "Why are you so afraid? Do you still have no faith?" They were terrified and asked each other, "Who is this? Even the wind and the waves obey him!" (Mark 4:35-41)*

The disciples knew Jesus Christ was with them in the boat when the storm broke. But they only called on Him when the boat was about to sink. Many of us know that we have Jesus Christ, the Name above every other name. Yet instead of calling on Him, we ignore Him. This is why we do not pray often.

Of course, there are those who misuse Him. There are many prophets and evangelists who use the name of Jesus Christ just to make money. Judas Iscariot was one of the chosen twelve disciples. He ate with Jesus Christ and was even the treasurer. According to Acts 1:16-20, God had already prophesied that his ministry would be taken over by someone else. When he failed to use what God gave him, it was taken away from him. I pray that God will not take Jesus Christ away from you.

> *Do not cast me from your presence or take your Holy Spirit from me. Restore to me the joy of your salvation and grant me a willing spirit, to sustain me.*
> *(Psalm 51:11-12)*

Many of us have abused the Gift or ignored the Gift. Many of us have cheapened the Gift. We can ask for restoration, right away. If you have not received the Gift, you can choose to receive the ultimate of all precious gifts today.

SHOW YOUR APPRECIATION

There are three ways to show that you appreciate a gift you have received. The first thing to do is to thank the giver, in a very big way. Of course, there are various ways of saying "thank you". There is a way you can say "thank you" to get rid of the giver.

The second way to show your appreciation is by telling others about the gift. You can keep on talking about the gift, either to show off or to inspire all your listeners to thank the giver on your behalf.

The third way you can show your appreciation is to use the gift appropriately so that the giver would be delighted. God has given us a great Gift – God the Son. We can show our appreciation by always saying "thank you". This was what David said:

> *Praise the LORD, O my soul; all my inmost being, praise his holy name. Praise the LORD, O my soul, and forget not all his benefits – who forgives all your sins and heals all your diseases, who redeems your life from the pit and crowns you with love and compassion, who satisfies your desires with good things so that your youth is renewed like the eagle's. (Psalm 103:1-5)*

> *I will extol the LORD at all times; his praise will always be on my lips. (Psalm 34:1)*

> *But as for me, I will always have hope; I will praise you more and more. My mouth will tell of your righteousness, of your salvation all day long, though I know not its measure. (Psalm 71:14-15)*

The second thing you can do is to let others know that God has given you a precious gift. You can let the world know that you are so wrapped up in this grand Gift that you and the Gift are one. That means you belong to Jesus Christ and that you are born-again. You can let people know that Jesus dwells in you or that He lives through you – that you are now a child of God.

> *I will sing of the LORD's great love forever; with my mouth I will make your faithfulness known through all generations. (Psalm 89:1)*

> *Sing to the LORD a new song; sing to the LORD, all the earth. Sing to the LORD, praise his name; proclaim his salvation day after day. Declare his glory among the nations, his marvelous deeds among all peoples. For great is the LORD and most worthy of praise; he is to be feared above all gods. (Psalm 96:1-4)*

LET YOUR LIGHT SHINE

The third thing you can do to use this Gift appropriately is to shed light. We know that Jesus Christ is the Light of the world.

> *While I am in the world, I am the light of the world.*
> *(John 9:5)*

If you receive the Gift of Light, you will become light yourself. What do you do with this light?

> *You are the light of the world. A city on a hill cannot be hidden. Neither do people light a lamp and put it under a bowl. Instead they put it on its stand, and it gives light*

> *to everyone in the house. In the same way, let your light shine before men, that they may see your good deeds and praise your Father in heaven. (Matthew 5:14-16)*

When you begin to shine with this Light, the glory will go back to the One who gave you Jesus Christ.

SHOW OTHERS THE WAY

We know that Jesus Christ is the Way, according to John 14:6. When you receive Jesus Christ, it follows immediately that you now know the way to Heaven.

> *Follow my example, as I follow the example of Christ.*
> *(1 Corinthians 11:1)*

Paul was saying that he had discovered the Way. While he would be walking along this Way, he would invite as many as will follow him, so that they could reach the heavenly destination together. If you receive the Way, you must lead others in the way to Heaven. You must lead them in the way of holiness, purity and by example.

INTRODUCE THE SAVIOUR

When you receive Jesus Christ, you have received the Saviour.

> *She will give birth to a son, and you are to give him the name Jesus, because he will save his people from their sins. (Matthew 1:21)*

The moment you receive the Saviour, what should you do? You are to point others to the Saviour and spread the word.

> *Salvation is found in no one else, for there is no other name under heaven given to men by which we must be saved. (Acts 4:12)*

Before we received Jesus Christ, we used our brains to reason. We wondered how there could be only one way to Heaven? (Usually represented in our minds by the big, big skies.) Your brain will tell you that it does not make sense. However, once you receive Jesus Christ, suddenly, you will understand why Jesus Christ is the only acceptable Way.

MINISTER HEALING

When you receive Jesus Christ, you have received the Healer. According to 1 Peter 2:24, we know that by His stripes, we have been healed. Once you receive the Healer and He dwells in you, He expects you to lay hands on the sick and transmit His healing power to make them well. That's the way you bask in the light of His awesome omnipotence.

> *And these signs will accompany those who believe: In my name they will drive out demons; they will speak in new tongues; they will pick up snakes with their hands; and when they drink deadly poison, it will not hurt them at all; they will place their hands on sick people, and they will get well. (Mark 16:17-18)*

When you receive the Healer, you have a healing ministry. Your job is to lay hands on the sick and stand aside and let the Almighty God do His work.

PROCLAIM PEACE

When you receive Jesus Christ, you have Peace.

> *For to us a child is born, to us a son is given, and the government will be on his shoulders. And he will be called Wonderful Counselor, Mighty God, Everlasting Father, Prince of Peace. (Isaiah 9:6)*

God expects you to go forth proclaiming peace – living peacefully everywhere you go.

> *How beautiful on the mountains are the feet of those who bring good news, who proclaim peace, who bring*

> *good tidings, who proclaim salvation, who say to Zion, "Your God reigns!" (Isaiah 52:7)*

Many Christians are troublemakers instead of trouble-shooters. They are agents of fear instead of Ambassadors of Peace. A child of God is expected to proclaim peace. Peter said to the man at the Beautiful gate that he had neither silver nor gold, but what he had he would give (Acts 3:1-8). He had Jesus Christ and he gave the man the healing power of Jesus.

If you have never received Jesus Christ, the free Gift of God, it's time to do so now. Come, taste and see that the Lord is good. If you have already received the Gift, you can do the three things we have enumerated above: thank Him, tell others about Him and use the Gift appropriately. Glory to God!

About the Author

ENOCH ADEJARE ADEBOYE became the General Overseer of the Redeemed Christian Church of God in 1981. The church has experienced unprecedented growth since he became the spiritual and administrative head. Under his leadership, the Church hosts a monthly prayer vigil on the first Friday of every month. The prayer meeting, which attracts about 500,000 people per session, is held at the headquarters in the Redemption Camp, on the outskirts of Lagos, Nigeria. Similar meetings are held bi-annually in the United Kingdom and the United States, where the Church has a strong presence.

God led Pastor Adeboye to establish "model parishes" – a vehicle which has not ceased to convey youth into the Kingdom, in large numbers. The church now has over four million members in about three thousand parishes all over the world.

By profession, Pastor Adeboye is a mathematician who holds a Ph.D. in Hydrodynamics. He lectured at the University of Lagos, Nigeria for many years. Renowned not only for the uncommon anointing of God on his life as a Pastor and International speaker, he is also a prolific writer. He has authored many titles used by God to touch lives. He is married to Pastor Foluke Adeboye and they are blessed with four children.

www.ingramcontent.com/pod-product-compliance
Lightning Source LLC
LaVergne TN
LVHW021549080426
835510LV00019B/2454